PRAISE FOR HEALING

"Right now we are in a state of such collective and continuous trauma that many of us can hardly imagine what being healed might look like at an individual level, much less as a people, as a society. This book is full of crucial survival tools that guide us in caring for ourselves and each other in ways that generate a world in which trauma is not our norm or our reason for coming together. Let this book heal you and grow your capacity to be a part of a healed future."

—adrienne maree brown,
author of *Emergent Strategy* and *Pleasure Activism*,
co-host of "How to Survive the End of the World"

"At this stage of the assault we see on black life, this book is a beacon, a light and a call, to take care and, more urgently, take self care. We need you to show up, but most importantly we need you to show up well rested. Dr. Joi D. Lewis reminds us of this call with such elegance and fierceness you can't help but be shook."

—Keno Evol, executive director of Black
Table A   erence

"Dr. Joi's work has profound   slow,'
as I continually put into pra   d over
the years, I've experienced a deep healing in my ___ . wish I
would've known has always been accessible to me. This is the much needed work on our journey to collective liberation."

—Joe Davis, poet, educator,
cultural architect, JoeDavisPoetry.com

"If you need examples on how healing is a justice issue, you've picked up the right book."

—Kabir Mohamed, founder of the daily desi vlog

"I have often said 'Freedom is not a secret. It's a practice.' The same could be said for JOY! In this book Dr. Joi offers tangible practices to show up for our own joy through the variable and often difficult circumstances we all face. This book is good medicine that doesn't expire."

—**Dr. Alexis Pauline Gumbs,** founder, Brilliance Remastered

"This book provides practical methods for healing, which are helping me to become a more authentic leader."

—**Leslie Redmond,** NAACP president, Minneapolis chapter

"What a fantastic, straightforward, and honest book. Dr. Joi challenges us in the most gentle and necessary way. *Healing: The Act of Radical Self-Care* is game-changing."

—**Suzanne Koepplinger,** director of the Catalyst Initiative, the Minneapolis Foundation

"Dr. Joi draws from her deep inner well of wisdom, with the grace of struggle, to share insights for healing ourselves and our communities together. OM offers a path forward for wondering hearts seeking to connect our inner lives with our collective lives to build hope and possibility for all of us."

—**Roberta "Bobbi" Cordano,** president, Gallaudet University

"Dr. Joi's words are needed more than ever. She shows not only how oppression hurts even the oppressor but also how healing is necessary to do the work our world requires."

—**Sean Kershaw**, St. Paul Public Works director

"To practice self-care is a political act rooted in deep love for oneself and the community. The Orange Method has taught me to show up for myself so I can show up for the movement, because we deserve liberation in the here and now."

—**Estefania Navarro**, community organizer, Unidos MN

HEALING

Healing

The Act of Radical Self-Care

Dr. Joi Lewis

ISBN: 978-1-63489-363-3

Printed in the United States of America

First hardcover edition: 2018
First paperback edition: 2020

24   23   22   21   20   5   4   3   2   1

Cover design by Jena Holliday
Interior design by Kim Morehead

Wise Ink Creative Publishing
807 Broadway St. NE, Suit 46
Minneapolis, MN 55413
www.wiseink.com

To order, visit www.itascabooks.com or call 1-800-901-3480. Reseller discounts
available.

For all the emotional laborers—invisible, acknowledged, compensated, unpaid—thank you for your commitment and hard work, and for inspiring me to write this book

Contents

Preface to the Paperback Edition

May the Revolution be Healing . . .

May it include freedom from diseases like diabetes, heart disease, and high blood pressure (which I call "high Black pressure"). They claim these diseases are hereditary, you know, passed down from generation to generation. Well, I guess. I am Black and I have high blood pressure, and my dad was Black and he had it, and his mother was Black and she had it, so I guess that's hereditary. But I think my point here is that the common denominator is that we are all Black, hence my conclusion is that high blood pressure is really high Black pressure. Perhaps its real cause is the weight of generations of oppression-induced racial trauma.

It is early July of 2020.

I am writing this preface to the paperback edition of *Healing: The Act of Radical Self-Care* in the midst of the COVID-19 pandemic, which has—in devastating and heartbreaking ways—exacerbated already existing oppression-induced inequities based on race, class, gender, disability, etc.

I am writing this preface from my home in Saint Paul, Minnesota, eleven miles from the Cup Foods in Minneapolis, where George Floyd was murdered by a police officer less than two months ago; there is still no justice for George Floyd. As of the printing of this book, there is still no justice for Breonna Taylor #sayhername, #prayhername, who was killed in her own home in Kentucky. The tide is changing, though. Mr. Floyd's brutal murder has triggered massive protests against racial injustice and anti-Blackness throughout the US and the world. A new law named for Breonna Taylor will ban no-knock warrants in Louisville, Kentucky. There is much work ahead, and I believe that radical self-care will light the pathway to a newly imagined world.

Please know, to quote Chani Nicholas, *the revolution will be healing!*

With peace and light,

"Dr. Joi" Lewis

Introduction

Radical Self-Care: the intentional practice of attending to your mind, body, and soul in ways that oppose the forces of oppression that want you exhausted and sick.

Dear one, I come spreading good news: choosing to be on a journey of healing is a radical act of self-care. It is possible for us to be free, laugh loud, eat well, raise hell, cry hard, say no, say yes, jump high, lay low, have boundaries, and be connected. We are worth all of this—and this is radical self-care. This is the core strategy for achieving well-being in the context of community, and for healing from emotional and historical trauma. Even in the face of all that is hard in the world, in the community, and in your life, you get to heal.

Life is challenging for many, including me, as we grapple with oppressive policies, increasing inequality, state-sponsored violence, and a rise in suicide. We are struggling. I have been aware of my own struggles with going numb and checking out when faced with the cruelty of this world. I needed a process, a tool, a solution to help me show up and get present, stay connected, and reach for my humanity and yours.

I lost my mom to cancer when I was seven months old and was raised by my dad. My siblings and I were always surrounded by a village. I have seen my fair share of heartache but have also experienced abundant joy. I know well the need for support systems and access to joy in a country that perpetuates trauma.

I grew up in East St. Louis, Illinois, only thirty minutes from Ferguson, Missouri, where Mike Brown was shot and killed. I currently live only ten minutes from where Philando Castile was murdered outside of St. Paul, Minnesota. Both East St. Louis and St. Paul (specifically my neighborhood, Frogtown) are important places for cultivating the ability to hold the contradictions of joy and pain.

Since the 2014 shooting of Mike Brown, the rallying cry against racism in the US has grown louder. After Ferguson, the Minneapolis Foundation raised public concern about civil unrest erupting in Minneapolis. I was contracted along with an amazing friend and colleague to facilitate conversations and hold space for seemingly disparate members of the community: city officials, including staff from the mayor's office, the chief of police, and the city attorney; Black Lives Matter activists; and Black community organizations like the NAACP and Neighborhoods Organizing for Change.

I've worked with city and nonprofit organizations and the Department of Justice. When Jamar Clark was killed in North Minneapolis in 2015, my firm, Joi Unlimited, along with the Diaspora Healers Network, provided healing spaces and facilitated difficult conversations. When Philando Castile was killed, Black Lives Matter–Minneapolis activists were gathered in my dining room. As we witnessed the murder on Facebook Live, we connected in a healing circle to express our grief, rage, and frustration. I regularly connect with teams of healers to convene healing space in the Twin Cities' community, around the country, and around the world, sometimes in person and sometimes virtually. For the last three years, the need continues to grow, as phone calls and texts come in daily, sometimes by the hour. As the rallying slogan of the student movement and second-wave feminism from the late 1960s states, "The personal is political." The folks I work with are not merely clients; they are my people, my family, because we are all connected, each of us.

Although I am a facilitator of liberation, space holder, healer, and light worker, I have sometimes experienced moments of hopelessness and paralysis after getting a call about a loved one struggling with mental health or contemplating self-harm, reading another story about an innocent community member being shot, or learning about yet another oppressive policy threatening our civil liberties.

I've had numerous moments where I've wondered, *How are we supposed to live with this kind of heartbreak?* So I wrote this book as a balm, a healing salve which is an offer for us not to simply bury our heads and curl up in a ball but, rather, to be intentional about what we need to live fully in this complicated world. It is not about highlighting the things we do that make us feel bad about ourselves but, rather, about noticing, being mindful, and seeing if we can develop or return to "practices" that we can use to heal us now and for our greater yet to be. It is not about saving the world but, rather, about reclaiming our humanity in community. This book is not full of answers, nor does it have a surefire recipe for changing your life or the world. It is full of perspectives, stories, practices, remedies, and recommended rituals. It describes a set of practices I created as an offering, a foundational process for radical self-care; I call this process the Orange Method (OM), and I will describe it more fully in the next chapter. This book will help you realize that joy and pain run from the same faucet.

For some, this book will be a return to a ritual and practice, and for others it will be a beginning of ritual and practice for the kind of radical self-care that leads to healing. It is about self-care that is healing—and that is indeed radical. This book is for you and your community, organization, and institution. It is written for me and for you.

I want these chapters to speak to you—the facilitator of liberation, the motivated seeker, the visionary leader, the exhausted executive, the isolated transplant, the seeking sojourner, the wounded healer, the progressive organization, the follower of light. Maybe you have gotten off track and are feeling the weight of the world. Perhaps you're fighting discouragement.

Throughout *Healing: The Act of Radical Self-Care,* I will use story and narrative to pull from the past and bring us to the present moment. I'll suggest some ways we can dream of what can be, of endless possibilities, while holding the contradictions of joy and heartbreak. Like me, you might be an instrument for illustrating both the struggle and possibility of healing. You need radical self-care to keep showing up and to continue breathing through the journey you are on and the pathway ahead of you.

This book is for each of us who are trying to figure out how to heal and take care of ourselves in a world of increasing heartache and despair. It includes tragic stories, some of which you will likely find quite upsetting. There are also stories that will bring laughter, joy, and hope. This book will invite you to show up, face that heartbreak, and also access joy. I want us to have a simultaneously intimate and public conversation about how historical and present-day trauma might show up in our lives (through addiction, an inability to get out of bed, isolation, etc.) so that we don't feel like it's just us and don't feel bad about how hard it is to think about and take care of ourselves. I also offer you some reminders that may be useful as we start to reconnect with our own and each other's humanity.

This book is not a history lesson about trauma (for that, I recommend Dr. Joy DeGruy's profound work, *Post Traumatic Slave Syndrome: America's Legacy of Enduring Injury and Healing*) or a scientific one (for which I recommend Dr. Bessel van der Kolk's *The Body Keeps the Score: Brain, Mind, and Body in the Healing of Trauma*). It is not about social movements or how they can be organized to change ourselves and the world (check out the amazing adrienne maree brown's *Emergent Strategy: Shaping Change, Changing Worlds*).

This book is about using our connections with one another to promote personal and systemic transformation. Changing ourselves and changing our world will take all of us thinking, working, and healing together. As my grandmother always said, "None of us are as smart as all of us."

As I write this from my home in St. Paul, Minnesota, on a cold winter morning in January, tears stream down my face. My blood pressure is very high (a persistent reminder that radical self-care for me is not a luxury, but indeed a matter of life and death). I am angry, shocked, and disappointed. Yet, at this moment, I am resisting the urge to shut down my computer. I'm resisting shutting my eyes and certainly shutting my heart. I need to keep writing because this message is important for me and for you.-

Writing *Healing* has given me the resolve to keep showing up for my own radical self-care and has lit the path to my own healing.

Chapter 1

A Framework for Healing

Radical self-care requires your ultimate health,
not just your ultimate sacrifice.

Welcome OM!

We live in an ever-changing local and global community impacted by abundance, injustice, opportunities, and trauma all at once. There are mass shootings, ecological disasters, police-involved murders, fatal hate crimes, political infighting, wars, and rumors of wars. Many of us feel hopeless and in deep despair, which often leads to addiction. Really awful things, like oppression and trauma, keep getting in the way of our ability to live in our fullness and reach for each other's.

Many of us feel exhausted because tragedy keeps striking and the trauma is so insidious that it feels like there is no relief. We want something to reach for. We are drowning in sorrow, yet we can see the shore of humanity and healing, so we keep coming up for air. Racial injustice has become the norm and is even acceptable in public spaces and perpetuated freely by public leaders. Everyday life is infused with fear, and it feels like there are no safe places anymore.

Places of worship are being bombed. It's scary to let your children (particularly, our Black, Brown, and Indigenous children) leave the house for fear that they may be stopped, harassed, stolen, or even killed.

We have the amazing technology of the internet, social media, smartphones, and chat rooms. Yet we are more disconnected and isolated than ever before. The world we live in is calling my message forward—with our urgent need for both intimate and public conversations about our heartbreak and healing. The message is needed on the street corners and in the White House, in homes, schools, places of worship, community gatherings, conferences, and book clubs.

In *Healing*, I offer a framework for holding the contradictions of joy and pain and engaging in individual and collective practices that will help you have space for both healing and heartbreak. If you turn away from the heartbreak and shut it off by numbing yourself or thinking you can avoid it, you are also turning off your access to joy. *Healing* exposes the truth: your mental and emotional health challenges are not your fault, and looking directly at the heartbreak will actually enable you to feel more joy. The world and systems of oppression were designed to crush your spirits and then to blame you for your responses to it. Oppression manufactures trauma.

As a facilitator of liberation, I also identify as a community and cultural healer. My work is grounded in the notion of healing justice, and it is from this framework that I do my work in the world—and in this book. As Cara Page and Susan Raffo wrote in a healing justice document for the 2014 US Social Forum, a healer is "someone who works with both the individual body and the collective body towards shifting patterns that cause disconnection." I am a bodyworker for the individual body (the whole self: mind, body, and spirit) and the collective body (systems, institutions, organizations). I gently press and dig deep to find the places where energy needs to be acknowledged, shifted, held, and perhaps released.

This is what radical self-care looks like.

I know that we have the collective wisdom in our spirits, hearts, minds, and DNA to heal from historical and present-day trauma. But it is going to take all of us, and we have to return to ourselves, to each other, and to our ancestral ways of being in the process. You will have to mix that in with what you know in the present moment and also imagine yourself in the community in the future, being fully human. We will need to go back and go forward and notice that all we need is in our present moment.

In order to be in the present moment, we need to stay awake for every aspect of life: the joy, the pain, the heartbreak, the excitement, the boring, the unexpected, and the transformation. It is easy to appear awake but still be dead inside. We may drink, veg out on social media or Netflix, smoke, work too much, have a lot of sex, shop, use street or prescription drugs, or use food (my drug of choice). I think too many of us have come to believe that we and our communities have to settle and go along with the way it has always been or how we always remembered it. Together, we are going to learn how to fully reclaim our humanity and interrupt historical cycles of oppression. This work is about reminding us that we can do way better than going small, staying sick, and giving up. We are worth reaching for. It's also about returning to what is true—that we want to be well, get free, live big, and heal.

We are not lacking time, just using our energy poorly. We're going to talk about these things. We're also going to go on a healing journey together and practice radical self-care along the way. You might wonder: How do you avoid disappointment and heartbreak? Well, the key to healing isn't avoiding or blocking out those things, because in doing so we also block out the awe and wonder of life. A radical self-care practice encourages us to embrace it all.

This is how "orange" enters. Orange is the sacral chakra color. It is located in your lower abdomen and is the emotional center where transformation starts. It controls the reproductive system and stimulates the respiratory and digestive systems. It shows new possibilities and offers alternatives. Furthermore, orange is my favorite color. I expand the use of orange in OM to also evoke transformation and liberation of self and systems and to remind us of our need for healing and therapeutic spaces and our ability to become more human and to find more joy, even in the face of oppression-induced trauma.

Developing the Orange Method has helped me recognize that many of us are missing practices that create rituals to gets us on the journey to healing.

We want to heal, but we often do not consistently practice self-care. I am sure you have many practices and rituals in your home and work life that you might even do on a daily basis, even if you do not call them "rituals" or "practices." According to the Cambridge

Dictionary, a ritual is "a set of actions or words performed in a regular way" or "any act done regularly, usually without thinking about it." Some of us may have a ritual of sitting in front of the TV and eating dinner. This is not a practice that serves us best, but it is a practice. At work, you may engage in the practice of eating at your desk or not even eating lunch at all. What are the practices in your life that are serving you? What are the practices that are not?

When you hear the word *self-care*, you many think spas, manicures and pedicures, going to the gym every day, and eating organic foods. Those can be a type of self-care. But that is not exactly what I mean; what I intend to share is much deeper than that. My message is about self-care that is healing—and that is indeed radical. *Radical self-care* requires your ultimate health, not just your ultimate sacrifice, and is the act of declaring and demonstrating that you are worth exquisite care right now. It is forgiving yourself, loving yourself, showing up for yourself, and learning not to apologize for putting yourself first. It is interrupting the narrative that says self-care is about being selfish.

To that, I say, being selfish is not the problem; the problem arises when we are self-centered. Radical self-care is about you—but it is not about *only* you. Famed poet, writer, and queer activist Audre Lorde wrote, "Caring for myself is not self-indulgence, it is self-preservation, and that is an act of political warfare."

The system of oppression does not want us to be well. The system wants us sick, tired, exhausted, isolated, disconnected, desperate, and believing in scarcity. These are the conditions that allow us to turn on ourselves and on each other. The system of oppression wants us sick in mind, body, and spirit, because if we were well we would no longer want to collude with a system that oppresses us or others. This is why healing is a radical act of self-care. The more joy we access—through listening to music, running, jumping, playing, hugging, loving, eating, resting, praying, meditating, singing, crying, relaxing, and being connected—the easier it becomes for us to be gentle with ourselves and each other. A lot is at stake: your humanity and mine. So in order to heal, you must commit to radical self-care, for yourself and for your community.

Healing and self-care are justice issues that are inextricably linked. The Orange Method—which accelerates our journey of reclaiming our humanity and manifesting the world we want to live in now, today, and tomorrow—invites us over and again to enter in, return to, and go toward our own humanities and everyone else's.

The Orange Method has four practices, each having its own section in the book with chapters that illuminate specific directions and remedies related to each practice.

1. Meditation (get grounded)
2. Mindfulness (get present)
3. eMotional Liberation (get free)
4. Conscious Movement (get going)

I created the Orange Method after years of bearing witness to my own and others' struggle in the fight for social justice while losing ground in the battle of taking care of ourselves and then feeling defeated. I needed something that would fortify us, encourage us, and fill us up. OM is a process of transformation and liberation that mirrors the yoga tradition of knowing your limitations. Like yoga, the Orange Method encompasses the need for therapeutic spaces, healthy eating, surrender, rest, stretching, and—most of all—practice. The Orange Method helps individuals and institutions to transform against the backdrop of oppression-induced trauma. You can heal by creating boundaries at work and with loved ones, falling in love with self and community again or perhaps for the first time, and developing better access to the healthy expression of grief and pain. Similarly, yoga asks the student to detach, find self-acceptance, and face emotions with honesty. Transformation is only possible when we get to the core cause of our symptoms.

The Orange Method, combined with radical self-care remedies, offers us a start, one that is accessible to every human being who truly believes in transformation and liberation, particularly those of us who have been left out historically.

OM helps me remember that I am not alone. It helps me re-'member to breathe when I get calls in the middle of the night from folks struggling through trauma. I have witnessed activists, healers, creatives, seekers, and plain everyday folks shift their perspectives, grow their connections, and increase their ability to take deeper breaths. I've seen trauma loosen its grip on our necks, our hearts, and our humanity because we put the Orange Method into practice.

OM reminds us that we are each amazing, awesome, and brilliant, and that this is what is true about all of humanity even though we cannot always show it. This process is about healing our broken hearts.

I want this book to help create an OMie nation, a community committed to holding space all over the world for radical self-care and healing—the kind that allows us to handle heartbreak. One of my favorite quotes—often credited to Rumi, the thirteenth-century Persian poet—says, "Perhaps your heart keeps breaking so it will stay open." As OMies, we advocate for the kind of radical self-care that allows us to rest but not quit and that requires us to get out of isolation and enter a community. The kind that empowers everyday life to be a meditation and transforms the things that are meant for our demise into a praise song. We are here for all of it.

~

Systems of oppression have programmed voices in our heads that say that we are not good enough, and OM uncovers those pesky recordings. Those systems are designed to keep us separated from each other and disconnected from our own humanity. Oppression is what ails us. Oppression is insidious, and the system is set up to make us feel like our struggles are simply our fault when, in fact, things happened to us and to our people and our ancestors before that. The Orange Method replaces those thoughts with the truth: we are powerful beyond measure. This is what makes OM's self-care radical.

Radical self-care is a direct action of resistance to the oppressive system that wants to keep you crushed, disconnected, addicted, numb, desperate, and in despair so you will turn on yourself and on each other. It is virtually impossible to be awake, well, present, rested, and connected to yourself and community *and* do the awful things that are required to act out your oppressor patterns. Carrying out acts of cruel and unjust treatment and control requires us to be numb, unwell, self-centered, and scared. We have to shut down our humanity in order to be oppressive. OM is an antidote for oppression. It is a salve for personal and collective liberation that eradicates the need for you to turn on yourself and do self-harm and encourages you to take exquisite care of yourself. It empowers you to move through the world knowing that you, like every human being, are amazing, awesome, and brilliant.

The Orange Method is not a destination; it is a process made up of daily practices that you can return to again and again. Each time I cry about something, I pause and practice OM as a way to be gentle with myself and to notice and allow myself that moment. It is not linear, neat, or easy, but it is healing. As you read this book, I encourage you to take time to pause, breathe, and remember that you have everything you need for the process of true healing. Radical self-care is not a luxury. It is a salve for our broken hearts.

You might be one of the many I've met in my work who sometimes feel defeated. Though you might not be ready to give up on life, fighting for justice, shifting policy, or transforming communities, you might feel like it would be easier to quit. I get it.

You are often willing to do whatever it takes to make an impact on the world, but you sometimes have trouble actually getting yourself up. You can literally get stuck in bed, on the couch, or in front of the TV. The struggle is real. I hear you loud and clear because I have been there, and recently. *Healing* is designed to get you out of isolation, out of your head, out of our home, and out of shame and hopelessness. Remember, you are only as sick as your secrets, and together we have a chance at both individual and collective healing. Dear one, please know that all of you is welcome on this journey: your joy, pain, uncertainty, trauma—every bit of you is welcome.

As you read this book and long after, I want you to be able to hold both heartbreak and joy while you look directly at injustice—both the kind that comes from outside and the kind we've internalized—and tell it "Not today!" It does not get to win. Imagine yourself walking hand in hand with me and a large circle of coconspirators, your OMies, and shouting, "I believe that we will win!"

We are winning because we are healing as a radical act of self-care in community.

~

The Orange Method is a both loving and rigorous process that will require much of you. Healing is serious business, and it is freeing. The words in this book may cause you to feel overwhelmed. Take a minute to breathe deeply. OM asks a lot of you because you are that important, and your healing is that important. I want you to have a good picture of where you see yourself now and a picture of where you would like to be. This healing process is not about you becoming someone different but about you becoming more of who you were always meant to be. Again, you are amazing, awesome, and brilliant.

Trust yourself to be guided to where you need to be. Our lives are not always ordered (you'll read more about this is chapter 5, Find Calm in Chaos), so be as flexible through this process as you need to be.

I've included within each of the four practices of the Orange Method what I lovingly refer to as OM remedies. They are outlined at the end of each chapter. These remedies were created to radically shape your self-care rituals. I imagine you might already be familiar with breathwork, meditation, and energy work. These remedies are an expansion, not a replacement of some of the self-care practices you're already using. I hope you will adopt the remedies that make sense for you and interchange them as needed. I expect you to add texture to your favorite remedies informed by your own experiences, life, and journey.

⌒

Recently, I participated in a healing circle that centered around one of my OM coaches, a young Latinx woman who had recently been detained by ICE. The circle was holding space for her and also for me, as my father had passed away several weeks before. We were both in tender places and grieving. As we always do in my healing circles, we began by inviting breath into our beings as a way to stop and pause. Next, we invited the ancestors into the space so that we would remember that we were not alone or limited by this physical world. Likewise, I invite you, dear one, to pause, take a breath, and notice that you are not alone.

Finally, consider who you would also like to invite into this moment on this journey —ancestors, fellow travelers, or anyone you would like to hold close in your heart—and who you would like to lovingly detach from as you begin this next step toward your healing.

Practice 1

Meditation

(Get Grounded)

Chapter 2

Start Where You Are

"I meditate. I burn candles. I drink green tea, and I still want to smack some people."
—Anonymous

First, I invite you to start where you are. It might not be pretty, but it's okay if you feel a little raggedy. The fact of the matter is that you are amazing, awesome, and brilliant exactly as you are right now. It's not "game over" because you feel depleted. Maybe you have done all the things that are highlighted in the quotation above but are still feeling disconnected or numb. Those feelings don't change the fact that you are amazing, awesome, and brilliant. Starting where you are might mean something as simple as having an extra glass of water today, parking a little farther from your office door, letting that call go to voicemail, asking for a hug, eating the celery that comes with the chicken wings, flossing your teeth, or putting on some lotion. Taking any action, even a small one, is choosing you—and that is where healing and radical self-care begin. They start with you.

As I've met people on my healing journey, I've learned that a force—the Universe, God, Nature, the Divine, whatever you want to call it—offers us infinite opportunities to return to the basics. Because I am a yogi and a healer, I automatically go to yogi speak when we begin our work. I'm here to tell you that *namaste* can wait. We are calling forth this spirt and standing on principles like *àṣẹ*, a philosophical concept through which the Yoruba of West Africa conceive the power to make things happen and produce change. I invite you to find some stillness first. Notice your feelings as you contemplate your needs. You might feel tentative or in conflict, or you might feel relief mixed with anxiousness. I invite you to integrate these feelings without letting them take over.

There is no end to this journey; it is cyclical. This is why I felt drawn to the circle, the sun like symbol on the book's cover—because it is not an ending but rather a continuum, an expansion. Investing in your healing and radical self-care is worthy of praise. I am cheering loudly for you, and I want the entire universe to know that you are worth celebrating, embracing, and loving. Reading these words is a testament that you've chosen to make healing and radical self-care your priority, so you're already winning. I encourage you to consider being completely pleased with yourself right where you are, in this moment, with nothing to change and nothing to alter. Allow yourself that feeling of deep self-love and appreciation—not for engaging in a performance, but just for showing up for yourself. That counts.

As you notice where you are, I want you to consider being gentle with yourself. Feelings will come up, and I trust that you will discern between fear and resistance. Although they both may bring up feelings of anxiousness at first, they metabolize differently in our body and spirit. *Fear* often causes you to freeze or become stymied. *Resistance*, when recognized, can be used as fuel. Like a plane that takes off against the wind, we can use resistance to move us forward. As a runner, I often have to remind myself of this principle of "moving forward" against the resistance. Why? Because when it is time for me to go for a run, I do not want to do it. I feel resistance. I am always the most tired that I have ever been in my entire life, and something in my body hurts, and I suddenly feel the need to wash dishes (which I hate), vacuum (I don't like to vacuum, either), or cook a five-course meal. I want to do anything else but go for that run.

My attitude is worse than bad when it's time for me to exercise. Trust me when I say that I am not a great person to be around the moments before going for a run. But slowly, the Orange Method is teaching me to honor my commitment to my own radical self-care. Maintaining good health is a decision, not a feeling. When I notice resistance, I pause and take a minute. I'm gentle with myself. Never once after a run have I said, "I wish I hadn't done that." I've never regretted spending those first five minutes of my day meditating or thought it wasn't worth it to eat healthy foods. I am glad to benefit from the practices that serve me. One of my former yoga teachers used to say, "If you are struggling, you are on the right path." Cleary I am on the right path, and resistance helps me to know that.

If you do have a sudden urge to move and get those feelings out, check out YouTube videos of the Drake and Shiggy "In My Feelings" challenge. It helps me to get moving and shift those feelings.

What I am learning over and again is that healing is much less about doing and much more about being—being present, awake, still, and in your feelings. Self-doubt, worry, and fear are not the way out; they are sometimes the way in. Sometimes they are all we have. OM shows us how to metabolize those things that sometimes seep into the crevices of our mind, body, and spirit and get them up and out as soon as possible. Eventually, through the practice of returning home to ourselves, we will get more comfortable with living fully in our bodies, and things that do not serve us will not be able to get in.

Growing up, I was taught to eat everything on my plate. My family had me stop and think about others who did not have what we did. They were coming from a good place. But now I realize that it was all going to become waste anyway, and it did not need to travel through my body first. I didn't have to be a human garbage can. As my wise Aunt Mossie says, the important thing to learn is how much to put on your plate in the first place. That's the real key to not wasting food and not eating more than one needs. The same is true of negative energy, self-doubt, and insecurities. They all need to be discarded. They do not need to travel through your mind, body, or spirit first.

Allow yourself to start where you are, as it will give you access to moving forward on things, even when the conditions are not perfect or you are afraid.
You can learn to do things even when you're scared. I am right here with you, and so are the OMies.

As I write this, I'm at a Kemetic yoga teacher training in Negril, Jamaica. Although that might sound blissful, and on some level it is, this training feels like one of the hardest things I have ever done. Despite the promise of leaving behind cold temperatures of seven degrees below zero in Minnesota and heading toward temperatures in the eighties, I had doubts about coming. I kept hearing voices say, "Wait until you are in better shape, until you lose weight, until you are more centered, until, until, until." But I am here, right now, for me. I chose to start where I was. Even as I move my body into rigorous poses on my mat sprawled across white sands under a sapphire sky and blazing sun, I could be easily distracted by the fact that I am the oldest student here and the largest in body size by a lot. But, despite my self-doubt and discomfort, I've quieted those voices, and I'm choosing to enjoy the present moment. About fifteen of us from all over the world came to the training. I was blown away in a conversation I had on the first day with one of my fellow yogis, who I will call Kenya. She flew in from California, and I asked her if she lived there. She said, "No, I do not live anywhere but in my body." *Wow*, I thought. *That is living fully and being present.* Kenya's words really spoke to me. I've decided to make this retreat my pause because everything I need is here. When you pause lamenting, planning, and problem-solving, you can conjure up the ancestors and their strength. You remember that you can do whatever you have to. In the present, there are no barriers to access what you need.

Despite my and others' doubts about what my body could do, I completed the training strong and am now a certified Kemetic yoga teacher. I had to ground myself and quiet the "committee meeting" in my head that often decides to convene—completely unwelcome and uninvited, of course—when I am about to do something amazing. I started where I was, one pose at a time. I kept trying. I would fall out, then get back in and fall out and get back in. Imagine what it would it be like to give yourself permission to start where you are and own your power.

Starting where you are is a choice available to you. You get to decide to stop and embrace the present moment. Don't wait until all the other things are done. That imaginary time—when you have the perfect job, body, partner, or house—is right now. You might say, "Okay, I will not wait until things are perfect, but I will wait until I feel better or until my attitude changes." I will let you in on a little secret: a good attitude is not a requirement for showing up for yourself. You do not have to feel happy or wait until you want to go for a run, because you may never go. You get the full benefits by actually meditating, running, or doing inner work, no matter your mood, and none of the benefits if you only think about it but don't do it. For the record, this is healing.

Get Grounded OM Remedies for Starting Where You Are:

- **Take deep breaths**: When you feel burdened by exhaustion, the aftermath of a traumatic event, grief, loss, or overwhelm, take a series of long, deep breaths, and keep breathing deeply until you're able to slow down your breath and take longer and deeper breaths again.

- **Repeat an affirmation**: Consider "I am amazing, awesome, and brilliant." This is a great way to interrupt the negative self-talk that runs through your head, to replace the negative messages you've been taught about yourself. This is the way we begin to change our unconscious mind and become more loving and kind to ourselves.

- **Clear your space and protect your energy:** Burn sage, sweetgrass, or palo santo as a way to clear out negative energy and to invite in peace and light. They each have amazing healing properties. Keep a stone in your pocket, like an agate or hematite, both of which ground and protect, strengthen connections to the earth, and offer feelings of safety and security. They also remove negativity and prevent you from absorbing others' negativity. Agate dispels fear and is good for children and perfect for carrying with you when you need an extra dose of strength.

Chapter 3

Pause and Take a Minute

*"I believe in prayer. It's the best way we have
to draw strength from heaven."*
—Josephine Baker

Praying or meditating are ways to pause, but so is just being silent and breathing. My faith in a higher power, who I call God, and the spirits of my ancestors, all of whom live in me, , help me to pause and take a minute. You may be living in anticipation of what might be or regretting what has already happened. This can cause you to procrastinate or to strive for a perfection that doesn't exist. Remember, procrastination and perfection are both fear-based emotions. Perfection has a nice ring to it, and we proclaim ourselves perfectionists and pat ourselves on the back. Sorry, but I'm here to tell you that procrastinators and perfectionists are one in the same. The OM remedy, pausing and taking a minute, frees us from both of those orientations. It is so simple but it is not easy. There is so much power in the pause, that moment when we allow fresh air to fill up our lungs, to move through our body, to get to our brains. This is when the Orange in OM helps us, to move from our center.

Regardless whether you are reading this book for yourself or your organization, institution, or community, pausing is one of the best technologies available to us, particularly when we are trying to get our bearings.

Dear one, even if the world feels as if it's crashing around you, know that it is radical for you to even consider that you are worth taking care of—and that you matter. Pausing is about knowing that because you do exist and you are worth it. Pausing is an intentional decision that offers powerful energy. Pausing is about knowing, being, and remembering that you are worth exquisite care, love, and light.

This is true especially when the bottom falls out, like when you lose your job unexpectedly, your significant other moves out, your baby is stillborn, your loved one dies, a child is taken from their mother, the entire island is devastated by a hurricane, or your cousin is gunned down by the State.

Life as you know it shifts. How do you find the new normal? You pause and take a minute. You cry, you shake, you scream, you holler, you throw things, and then you pause and take a minute. Notice that you are still here and you can make it. You can heal from these heartbreaking things that happened to you and around you. You did not die, although it may feel like you want to. It's all very real and extremely devastating, yet you can find a new grounding. Healing is not a set of complex steps or the ultimate destination. It's a combination of committing to ourselves. It's adopting remedies that empower us to release all that doesn't serve us and to activate what does.

Recently, a client I'll call Dana sent me a list of things keeping her up at night. Dana is a busy mother of a toddler, owns a business, and was drowning in obligations, feeling overwhelmed, and struggling with burnout. Not to mention being exhausted from parenting and holding space for her staff, clients, family, and community with little to nothing left for herself. I sensed that Dana felt that peace and relief were beyond her reach and would require a complicated regimen of actions. Dana's circumstance is pretty common in a super intense world in which we are always plugged in. After taking a look at her short list, I immediately knew that simply pausing could make a world of difference. I told her to spend some time in a morning ritual, which is the grounding OM remedy I recommend the most when someone is struggling with overwork and overwhelm.

The OM morning ritual is important as the first thing you do when you wake up, before the committee meeting starts in your head—all those uninvited voices trying to get you to do their agenda for the day.

If you're feeling burdened by the weight of your pain, or like Dana, have burnout, beginning your day with the morning ritual can be the foundation from which you build your plan for healing and radical self-care. Simply pausing in the morning allows you to set an intention so you won't be pulled in all directions throughout the day and you don't react to everything that comes at you. Although you cannot control the many demands and expectations of others as you move through the day, you can start your day centered and grounded in what actually makes sense for you.

The process of healing through radical self-care is not so much about time management as it is about energy management. Pausing is an incredible energy audit. It enables you to check your "energy account" before the kids wake up, before you check your email, and before you tackle the first crisis. You will get clear about how much is in your energy account. The morning ritual sets you up to get what you need before you leave the house. It's a hefty deposit in your energy bank.

The last time I spoke with Dana, she pulled me into an embrace and shared that the morning ritual is now her grounding OM remedy of choice, and it had already begun to shift her sense of being. "Dr. Joi, I always thought my quiet time in the morning was productive until I realized I wasn't being intentional. I was focused on everyone else, heavy with what I knew my day could bring, and obsessed with preparing for the things that might surprise me. Now, some mornings I do two of the steps or one or all of them. Regardless, I start my day feeding my soul, not burdening it."

It may take a few tries, days, weeks, or months for you to get into a rhythm to pause and take a minute. The morning ritual helps you cultivate some compassion for yourself and others. It gives you some extra footing as the ground tries to settle when there are so many demands on you, your time, and your emotional labor.

Get Grounded OM Remedies for Pausing and Taking a Minute

- **Notice the tension.** Notice where tension is showing up in your body, and put a finger or palm there to bring you back to a grounded space, sending energy filled with peace and loving-kindness to those areas. Don't forget to breathe. Yes, right there, take that breath and another one for good measure. Nice and slow, there you go.

- **Find stillness.** If you have only a little time, find a spot on the floor in your home, in your office, at the gym, or on the grass, and lie down on your back. Let your hands lie face up next to your body, let your feet fall apart at the ankles, and let your head rest naturally with your eyes open or closed, whichever feels comfortable. This is shavasana (the dead body pose) in yoga. Lie there for two minutes. Try not to scratch, fidget or solve any problems; simply allow yourself *to be*. Those two minutes can give you a shot of energy. The more you can pause and take a minute or two on the mat, the more you can begin to do the same off the mat and not react to everything that comes at you.

• **Start with the morning ritual.** Begin your day with intention and use the morning ritual as the first activity you do when you wake up. If you can, complete your ritual before others in your home wake up and before getting on the phone to talk to others.

Possible things to include in your morning ritual

1. Pray

2. Meditate

3. Read two pages of a book that is uplifting (perhaps something spiritual, affirming)

4. Exercise for at least fifteen minutes as soon as you get up

5. Listen to an inspiring podcast.

6. Eat breakfast

7. Eat breakfast, pack your lunch, Prepare for dinner

8. Listen to your favorite music on the way to work

9. Stay in gratitude

10. List three people you want to text or call this week.

Practice 2

Mindfulness

(Get Present)

Chapter 4

Shift from Lies to Liberation

"I am no longer accepting the things that I cannot change, I am changing things I cannot accept."
—Angela Davis

Radical self-care and healing provide space for us to examine the impacts of oppression-induced trauma and how it can get internalized and cause us to turn on ourselves and each other. Whether you are its target or agent, oppression erodes our humanity. This OM remedy, shifting from lies to liberation calls us in to examine our numbness and helps us recognize how the narratives of popular media and social media have installed us with false programming and news about what is actually true. It invites us to stop and ask, "Is this true?" It helps us recognize the narratives we ingest about who is the villain and who is the victim.

This OM remedy interrupts the persistent effects of toxic stress and trauma we experience every day and creates more space for our work in the world and our broader lives. With such space, I believe we are able to gain access to deeper connections with ourselves and others and to have healthy expressions of grief, pain, and joy. The practice of radical self-care mirrors in some ways the practice of yoga, which asks us to explore our present limitations, detach, find self-acceptance, and face our emotions with honesty so we can reach for our own humanity and each other's. Our healing is also very much connected to exposing the lies that have been fed to us about who we are and who our people are. It's about knowing what we are capable of and acknowledging our limitless brilliance. It's about exposing the horrible things that have happened that may have caused us to adopt limiting beliefs about ourselves, beliefs that foster self-doubt and anxiety and put us in a mindset of scarcity. Limiting beliefs have limits: they can be interrupted. Oppression, internalized racism, and their coconspirators can be stopped. Healing and radical self-care usher in the liberation.

If you are committed to racial and social justice, it may be easy to show up for protests and rallies and speak out against injustice but more challenging to go about your day, living your life with your family and loved ones and coworkers. Like me, you may sometimes fall short and find yourself reproducing the kind of conditions you fight against.

What do you do every day when oppression
or internalized oppression shows up?

I'd like to share a personal story that illustrates how intense internalized oppression is.

When my partner and I moved into what is considered one of the best neighborhoods in the Twin Cities, only a few blocks from the governor's mansion, we had a false sense of "safety." The streets were lined with lots of trees, beautiful gardens, and plenty of playgrounds and greenspace. I never quite felt comfortable there, although the dominant narrative about living in a predominately white, upper-middle-class neighborhood told me to feel differently. The story goes, since there are so many white people and rarely any brown faces to see, this is a safe place. I am from East St. Louis, a city in which of 98 percent of residents are Black, so that is where I feel the safest.

Nonetheless, we developed a fondness for our home and tolerated the neighborhood. We were friendly with some of the neighbors, including the Black family next door. Our neighbors could easily see into the first floor of the house because, after years of being in a relationship with a white Jewish woman raised in suburbia, I had given in—we left all of the window treatments up. My friends have tried many times to revoke my Black card over that concession, saying things like, "You know that we're Black; we don't do that." Nonetheless, that's how my partner and I rolled: blinds up.

One summer night, there was a serious thunder and rainstorm, and my partner was hanging with our then two-year-old niece in the family room while I poked around the kitchen. All of a sudden, we heard loud banging on our back door, and it seemed like someone was trying to get in. I told my partner to grab our niece and move to the front of the house while I called 911. I was so scared because I had never had this experience before and this strange new neighborhood put me on edge. I told the police dispatcher that someone was trying to get into our house. The dispatcher asked me to describe the person. Without pause, I said that he was a Black man wearing a hoodie. My partner said, "Joi, you can't see the person's face; you don't know what race he is." I quickly recanted my description, horrified at my own internalized racism, but was still terribly scared about whoever was trying to get into our house. I was sweating profusely, pacing, and trying to listen. Now the person was banging on the front door.

I reported this to the dispatcher, and he said I should take a look out the peephole. That did not seem terribly safe, but I did it. Turns out it was our neighbor from across the alley, a friendly white man—I mean super white, like *Leave It to Beaver* white—who we often saw walking his dog. He was trying to get our attention to let us know we had left the garage door up. He was concerned about our things getting either ruined by the storm or stolen, as several burglaries had occurred in the neighborhood. I reported to the dispatch that it was our neighbor so that they could call off the search for another Black man that did not exist.

I am sure they would have found this nonexistent Black man and charged him, and I would have picked him out in a lineup. This is the pathology that racism produces. There I was, someone who had spent her entire adult life working for social justice and ending racism, and the moment I felt scared, I named a Black man as the perpetrator of a crime that was not even being committed. Black people are believable as villains, especially in white neighborhoods.

This event happened over ten years ago, and I am still devastated and embarrassed that I would ever do something like that. I wish I could say this was the only example of internalized oppression that I have experienced, but it is not.

I shared this story with you because we all must realize racism and other forms of oppression are insidious. Oppression gets swallowed and internalized and shows up in the strangest places. If you are filled with shame about places where you have colluded, been complicit, or turned on yourself or others you care for, you are not alone. Please remember that you are only as sick as your secrets, and find a trusted person with whom to share the secrets that feel the most shameful.

This is the way we heal from systemic oppression: by getting honest with ourselves and each other about the misinformation we have been forced to believe and internalize about ourselves and other people. I must admit I feel some shame bubbling up that this story will be out for folks to read. But it is important to get real, tell the truth, and invite all of us to stop pretending. This is my life's work, and I am deeply affected—and who among us is not? However, if you do not get honest and work on it, the lies will continue, and there will be no true liberation.

I am very practiced at understanding where I am the target of oppression, particularly around race, gender, and sexuality. However, I am less practiced at looking at my own oppressor patterns. In my workshops and retreats, I regularly provide an opportunity for folks to look at their multiple and intersecting social identities and to acknowledge where they are in the agent group, holding power and possibly running oppressor patterns. This is important work to do. I invite you to join me and look at what have you ingested and how is it coming out so that you can interrupt it and shift from lies to liberation.

Get Present OM Remedies for Shifting from Lies to Liberation:

- Find a few trusted friends, colleagues, or family members, and share stories of a time when you perpetuated or internalized oppression. Make a commitment to name your oppressor patterns and to interrupt them. Allow each person to share his or her story for five minutes (or however long you choose) without being interrupted. Ask everyone listening to remember that the person they are listening to is amazing, awesome, and brilliant and wants to heal from the pressure to collude with oppression. I recommend that this OM remedy be practiced with folks who share your same or similar intersecting social identities (race, class, gender, religion, sexuality, etc.). It takes a ton of emotional labor to do this work across differences, especially in the absence of a skilled facilitator of liberation, space holder, or healer. It can be a trigger and cause more trauma, so be thoughtful and kind, and ask for consent about the emotional labor you are asking someone to do.

- **Make a vision board.** Change the images and ideas in your head. Put together pictures on a board, on your wall, on your phone, or on your screen saver that deliberately and actively contradict the stereotypical images fed to us by the oppressive society. Read books and watch movies that offer real stories by and about people who have been historically marginalized that conjure up joy, show respect, and acknowledge resistance and resilience. Build real authentic relationships with people across differences. Do an inventory of who is really in your life, and expand your circle. Don't miss out.

- **Start a visualization practice**. Come to a comfortable seat, conjure up a memory of a person you respect from a group different from your own. Think about that person's life and accomplishments and about what you admire about the person. If your images involve only people who you don't know but who you admire on TV or in literary circles, that is a good start, but I encourage you to make connections with inspiring people from a variety of different backgrounds. Be a serious coconspirator and learn about others, speak up, and use your special powers for good.

Death by Invisibility
Dr. Joi Lewis

We died at least a thousand times before yesterday's bloody massacre.
Certainly at least ten times just this past week. It's like a death by a thousand paper cuts.
We queer bodies, stuffed in places too small to hold all of our humanity. Those places mostly are in small minds made especially for us to live.

We died a thousand times before yesterday's massacre, queer bodies, open season, year round.

We die when we go "home," like just before boarding the airplane and praying that your carry-on will fit in the bag tester.
You know it's too big but you pray that you will get a pass.
We stuff ourselves, shrink down trying to fit the dimensions of whatever love your heart can hold, a hug, a family dinner, an honorable mention of your partner by someone.

We died a thousand times before yesterday's bloody massacre, queer bodies open season, all year round.

We die when we walk into church in our Sunday best, dressed in respectability, hoping that the sermon will not be about us today—condemnation, Sodom and Gomorrah—a hell built just for us.

We died a thousand times before yesterday's bloody massacre.

We die almost every Monday when we go into the work place, and we pray that no one asks about our weekend.
We have run out of vagueness, trying to leave out any descriptors that mention our life with our partners.
We use just enough words to barely say anything.

We died a thousand times before yesterday's bloody massacre, queer bodies open season, all year.

We die every time our trans body has to use a public restroom.
We hope we can just get out alive.

We died a thousand times before yesterday's bloody massacre, queer bodies, open season, all year.

We die at the thought of our actual physical death.
Will our obituaries really tell our stories, or the ones our "loved ones" wish was our story?
Who will get to march in as family?
Will our tombstones be etched with the names we really go by.

Our repass does not take place in a church basement, but rather on Saturday nights at the club, like in Orlando, after so many of us are killed, emotionally and spiritually during the week.

Those places are sacred, a reclaiming of our humanity, we pour out libations for ourselves and our fictive kin, for the parts of us that died that week.
We spread the gospel of love, and walk out the door to the battlefield.

Even when we die, *we still do not get to be free. We get to still claim the right to be free.*

Chapter 5

Find Calm in Chaos

"Peace. It does not mean to be in a place where there is no noise, trouble or hard work. It means to be in the midst of those things and still be calm in your heart."
—Unknown

It is not uncommon for people to enter into my healing circles, workshops, retreats, or coaching sessions with strong feelings of not wanting to be there, not wanting to be anywhere, or not wanting to have to talk to other people or do any kind of activity, reflection, or engagement.

Some of those feelings may be kicking up for you as you read this book. You know those feelings of wanting to disengage, go away, watch TV, and shut it down. I get it. A lot is pulling at you to not be present, to recoil, and to disconnect. This strong desire to go away is often in part due to some historical trauma you or your people have experienced, and it can get triggered by present-day trauma.

You may feel pulled to respond in one of four ways often referenced in writings and discussions around trauma: fight, flight, freeze, or fawn. When things are chaotic and you find yourself having to constantly be "on," running from one intense incident to another, you may fight or flee from opportunities for self-care—if not physically, at least emotionally. But it is important to take time get filled up through a workshop, a retreat, or some other kind of professional development.

Attempting to find calm in chaos is indeed an act of radical self-care. It is about being open and not giving in to the urge to run or to stay and react in ways that may be harmful.

If you begin to hear voices in your head that are telling you to shut down or to lash out, know that many of us often feel like this.

At one of my workshops, a respected and usually vocal community member walked in the door. He was sullen and disconnected, a noticeable departure from his usual jovial and engaged demeanor. As a facilitator of liberation, I often encounter this heavy energy. After studying this phenomenon during my twenty years of holding space, I have come to understand it is trauma showing up. It is a reminder that I must find a way to hold space in order for people to find calm in chaos.

In all the workshops I facilitate, I set up the physical space to usher in a healing presence. Colorful batiks decorate the tables, an infuser emits lavender essential oils, and Nina Simone's lovely singing plays softly in the background. Books by authors such as bell hooks, Gloria Anzaldúa, Audre Lorde, Andrea Jenkins, and Pema Chödrön are spread out across the room. Healthy nourishing food and drinks are available for participants. If allowed, sage or palo santo is burning, and crystals and stones are spread about for protection. Large signs display "Community Learning Guidelines" and "Learning Foundations" to create brave space where all can feel welcome.

As soon as you enter into the space, you are welcomed and you can feel your energy shift, your shoulders relax, and your brow become less furrowed. You begin to find calm in chaos and some refuge from your hectic life, from the heartbreak in the world, from the latest tragedy you heard about on the radio or in your own life. This is not about decorating or trying to make things look cute; this is about ushering in joy and creating a contradiction to the hurt, pain, and ugliness. You come in and are welcomed with a smile, a hug if you consent, and an activity or OM remedy that helps you to get present in the moment and notice that for at least a short time you can find some refuge. There are activities that get you up and moving. We then gather in a circle and spend a short time in a guided meditation to get present. As the facilitator, I explain the circle and share the use of a talking stick, adopted from the sacred process of circle from the Indigenous People, who use a feather to ensure that everyone has a voice. I say, "We are now in circle. Whoever has the talking stick, it is their time to talk. Everyone else's job is as important or perhaps more important—to listen. When you get the talking stick, please say your name, and we will all say, 'Heeeey.'" I also ask a question such as "What is something that is important to you that we would not know by just looking at you? And "What is your hope for our time together today?" If time allows, we give everyone an opportunity to check in.

Orange Method(OM)

Orange Method Practice	Learning Outcome	Framework
Meditation	Get Grounded	Opening Welcome Introductions
Mindfulness	Get Present	Concentric Circles Radical Hospitality
eMotional liberation	Get Free	Radical Self-Care Vision
conscious Movement	Get Going	Dance/Yoga Break Closing Circle

I always use the OM facilitation process when I hold space. Why? Because it is a return to ritual; it becomes something that people can depend on. You know that no matter how intense the situation is, no matter how chaotic, the space will be set up for healing and you will get to speak and have time to breathe, cry, move, and hopefully even laugh. You will get a chance to really be listened to, and you will be reminded repeatedly by me and other participants that everyone there is amazing, awesome, and brilliant. I teach the OM facilitation process to organizations and institutions to create a practice of ritual for building a culture of healing and radical self-care in community.

The intention is to use these OM practices
during a healing circle in the hopes that you are reminded that
you can create a healing environment anywhere—whether you
are in your home, at your office, or in your car.

So when it was time for the brother who walked in with heavy energy to check in, he said, "I really did not want to come. I have too many things to do, and who has time for self-care when people are dying in the streets? Right before I came here, I was called to the scene of a homicide. The last thing I wanted to do was come to a meeting." After a long, deep sigh, and with tears in his eyes, he said, "I am so glad that I am here. I needed this more than I could have ever imagined. I have only been here for thirty minutes, but I feel so much better, because I gave myself some time to actually feel, to breathe, to be in community, to be held, and to be seen. Has it really been only thirty minutes?" Although he wanted to flee and not come to the healing circle, he came, and the environment allowed him to find some calm in chaos.

That shift is what I want for you—to take a few moments, breathe, and engage in some radical self-care. However, it does require some preparation. Healing and radical self-care are a marathon, not a sprint. You can't simply jump out there and do it, particularly when there is so much chaos. I ran the Twin Cities Marathon many years ago; it was on my bucket list, and I trained for months by regularly jogging and building up mileage. When I actually ran the marathon, provisions were available for me and all the other runners out there. There were water stations, paramedics, run marshals, roadblocks for cars, porta potties, people along the route cheering us on, and food and beverages at the end. Maybe you could go out and run 26.2 miles with no provisions set up for you, but I would not recommend it.

It's the same thing with healing and radical self-care: you want to prepare, build up a reserve, and understand the spaces you are going into. You want to cultivate your ability to not be bowled over by chaos. This happens when you engage repeatedly in activities that create space in your life to notice and connect and feel.

Every day, my loved ones, friends, colleagues, and clients express how chaotic things can sometimes feel. One of the consistent feelings my new coaching clients share before they start working with me is a deep sense of overwhelm. Perhaps you are having some of these experiences now: having trouble sleeping, missing important dates and details, having little time to eat and even less time to move your body. It's all understandable because you likely have so much demand for your time and attention. If you are worried about budget shortfalls, grant deadlines, meeting fund-raising goals, your kid getting bullied at school, making it home by a decent hour, or finding time to take a real vacation and unplug, finding calm is essential.

Yet, despite the chaos, you continue the work, because it's not about capitalism and simply amassing wealth. For you, it's about social justice and liberation, so you push yourself past what makes sense for your health and well-being. Radical self-care likely sounds like a nice luxury reserved for your five-day vacation once a year, if you're lucky. You really are starting to think it may not happen until you retire, if you can ever afford to do so. It can be hard to think through this kind of chaos. Many of the folks I work with share similar sentiments.

One of my clients—we will call her Candace—was an executive director of a nonprofit organization where she did amazing liberation work for girls. She was also the owner of a coaching business. When she started working with me, she too was stressed about so many obligations and pulls on her time. It felt like chaos. She had vision of becoming a powerful philanthropist who could directly provide resources to the social justice and liberation issues she cared about. However, because she was dealing with so much chaos, she was re-creating the same conditions of overwhelm in her coaching business that she experienced in her work as an executive director.

Since implementing the practices of OM, she has a strong morning ritual practice and has restructured her business model to support her own radical self-care and build a solid six-figure coaching practice. Be like Candace: implement some of these strategies, and start living your best life.

So much is at stake for you individually and in your community work, so you must find calm in chaos.

I hope that some of these OM remedies will allow you to get filled up and to track and notice where you are and what you need.

Get Present OM Remedies for Finding Calm in Chaos:

- **Hand-over-heart meditation.** When you find yourself in the middle of a chaotic moment, put your hand over your heart and allow your own hand to deliver the healing energy that is needed. You will begin to feel your entire nervous system calm down. There is so much healing power in your own touch. Be sure to use this as an opportunity to slow down your breathing. This is great to use when you first wake up and throughout the day when you need to invite some calmness into your heart and spirit. Try it for two minutes. It can alter your entire aura.

- **Create calming space.** You do not need to be in charge of facilitating a meeting or a retreat for others to create a space that is beautiful, welcoming, and calming. Pick a room in your home, or a corner of a room, and set it up with a few books or other pieces of art you find meaningful or inspiring, some fabric or other material, maybe a candle or two. Consider making an altar. Use an infuser to emit some healing fragrance from essential oils.

- **Journaling for calming.** This type of journaling can happen anywhere, and you'll want to have some prompts ready to get your attention away from the chaos. You can write the answers on your phone or on back of a napkin—it does not matter. Here are three questions you can have at the ready; put them in the note section of your phone so you do not have to remember them.
  1. What are three things that I love?
  2. What are three lines of my favorite song?
  3. What do I like to put in a calming bath?

The Repass
Dr. Joi Lewis

Last night over communal chicken
we gathered like at a repass after a funeral for our kin,
comforted by red beans and rice, and of course biscuits,
the fried chicken tasted like community
that we had not felt since those four little girls died.

We kept making room for each other
moving, tables and chairs
maybe as a distraction for our grief.

We never said out loud that we just left a funeral
or that in this season, we are in perpetual mourning,
tears flowing or simply dried up from weary eyes,
cried out from too much death and trauma.

Poetry readings have quickly become funerals where heart-wrenching
eulogies are delivered for Black lives taken too soon;
mothers are not supposed to bury their children.

It took us a while to know we were at a funeral.
Lots of hugging of friends and fictive kin we had not seen for a while
or maybe even yesterday,
but we live in a day when seeing Black faces again
are not at all promised
hugs turn in to long embraces
and the smiles on our faces begin to fade
as we realized the funeral was about to begin.

I am so glad I wore black
although there was no procession, it started to become clear
when we had marched in taking our seats,
minus the swaying of hips and clapping of hands
that our soul-wrenching music prompts us to do.
We were at a funeral;
we sat in the family section reserved for us with signs that said "Givens."

We knew when she began that this was a funeral for our kin—
our cousins, nephews, brothers, fathers, and sons.

Today the poetry reading was an uninterrupted eulogy.
I had never been to a funeral for ten people all at once.
I imagine this was what the ancestors did
after so many lynchings of Black bodies
untangled ropes from limp, lifeless bodies to be buried underground.

Funerals are rights of passages accelerated for Black bodies,
The genocide and mass murder of Black boys and men . . .
the shame of a nation

I feel like collapsing under the infinite descriptive words
of Black "boys and men's crimes of existing,"
of being born Black,
murder for a Black man contemplating breathing in this world
you simply die for even the thought of living . . .
heartbreak

Yet my heart still aches in those moments
when there is no mention of death of Black women and girls
or THE WALKING DEAD.

Some of us are being hung in the cool of the day
strung up out there for the whole world to see.
our Black bodies on display to be mocked, spat on, pillaged.

Black girl, backs to be rode like horses.
No, not on a black buck, but a Black girl child,
who gives a f***?
I smell a cover-up
of everything but our Black girl bodies,
because they are for the taking

Even our stories are simple rides to the next big thing
just another trick, a quick hit and move on.

No condom to protect us from the disease of oppression that you carry,

just deposits, no filter, straight into a body of knowledge
of our pain and suffering
it goes into the abyss.
Miss me with your omissions

You may not have noticed it—the headline that read:
"McKinney, Texas, pool party."
You can sometimes grab a newspaper they sell over there on the corner
at the intersection of sexism and racism;
then go down the road a bit in front of the store called homophobia

After you pick that up,
jump on the highway of female mutilation.
I know they outlawed it in Nigeria.
but they are way more progressive in third-world countries

In the West we don't . . . even acknowledge that we do female mutilation
there is no ceremony for it
unless you count rape or sex trafficking
then we are ceremonially rich

Razor blade on her tongue and God said don't
and I was for a second hopeful, but I knew they would cut out our stories
no pleasure in even the acknowledgment that we exist or existed
not even our death
well sometimes and honorable mention
it's as if we have no right to feel anything
it feels like they keep cutting out the clit
we are not supposed to feel
I just act simple minded on your behalf . . .

I am so thankful for the repass
the chicken is always sooo good
we don't even have to talk about the funeral
and sometimes there is twerking and dancing
other cousins just keep dropping by

`"Is that chicken I smell?"
we pour out some libations for those who are no longer with us

there is always plenty to share
that chicken multiplied like the fish and five loaves of bread
and at once we were no longer just fellows we became family!

Practice 3

eMotional Liberation

(Get Free)

Chapter 6

Remember It's Not Your Fault

"What's true is [that] trauma makes weapons of us. And fools, and secret keepers, and collaborators in harm. If we are going to grow, we must embrace truth telling . . . We must get more passionate about healing than we are about punishing."
—adrienne maree brown

There is no agency deployed to help us heal from the historical and present-day trauma and political heresy under which we are currently living. No systematic emergency response is available for any of us to deal with the erosion of our humanity that happens as we live with this personal and collective trauma. For many of us, the impact extends beyond posttraumatic stress disorder because there really is no "post"—the trauma continues. It's sometimes hard to understand fully the reality of the world we live in that gets reduced to sobering headlines, Facebook posts, and tweets that may include #BlackLivesMatter, #SayHerName, #Muslim, #MeToo, #FamiliesBelongTogether. These magnify again and again the calamitous effects of this never-ending cycle of trauma. The overwhelming feelings of shame can make you want to keep things to yourself—to not bother anyone, not be a burden, not tell any secrets, and not get people in trouble. Truth is, we are only as sick as our secrets.

Several deeply committed folks in our community—including activists and healers in the movement to reclaim our humanity— have committed suicide in the past few years. Right now, I hold space for and am aware of many more folks who are experiencing suicidal ideations, sleeplessness, depression, loss of appetite, and deepening addiction to substances that help them numb their pain. Self-harm is a huge concern. Unfortunately, I have borne witness to the kind of trauma that results in self-harm, including the ultimate form of self-harm. We are making progress, but we must continue to speak out against any kind of stigma around mental health. Mental health oppression is real; it is isolating, shaming, and actually dangerous.

One young sister, whom I will call Terri to protect her identity, was an activist for Black liberation and the movement to end violence against women, and she became caught in the intersections of these movements in a deep and complicated way. Terri was one of my students when I was a dean. She was a grad student, studying women and gender studies. Brilliant, brave, compassionate, generous, and just plain scary-smart. She was also a fierce community organizer, advocating for changes in laws for partner and intimate violence and rallying against police brutality aimed at Black and Brown men. She would often stop by my office and let me know what was happening on the front lines, explaining why it was important to organize. Being at the center of both of these movements left little time for Terri to engage in her own practice of radical self-care, to take some long-needed breaths, and to know she too was worth being cared for.

On an exceptionally cool day, Terri walked into my office bundled up with her face almost hidden under her hat and scarf. Her usual bright smile was gone, and her energy was heavy. She was always a very serious person; you knew she meant business, even though her smile was always warm. This day was different. Terri shared that she had gone on a date with a young man who she knew from movement work, and it was clear that they liked each other. She said they went out and had a really good time, and at the end of the evening, he asked if he could come in and hang for a while. She said sure. Things changed once they arrived at her place, Terri said his energy shifted, and he became quite forceful in his tone and body language. She asked him to leave, but he wouldn't. He started grabbing and pushing and kissing her. Although she said stop many times, he would not take no for an answer, and he raped her. She reported being in shock and not being able to move. He kissed her on her cheek—and left as if nothing happened.

Terri said she told her roommate and was encouraged to call the police, but she could not do it. We talked about it, and she said that although she knows that he was wrong and she feels traumatized, she cannot bring herself to report him to the police because she knows what happens to Black men when they get involved the justice system. "Dr. Joi, this is my life's work," Terri said, "but I also know what happens to women on the other side of violence from men, and I do not know what to do. I cannot tell anyone else about it. I cannot tell the police, and I cannot talk to a therapist. I just need to forget that it happened and live with the secret. I will be alright."

I connected her to a therapist and to the crisis hotline for sexual assault and violence, but she said she needed a moment and reiterated that she could not see herself reporting him. There had to be some restorative justice process. After Terri left, I called and checked on her. Her roommate told me she made it home safe and was sleeping.

The next day, early in the morning, the roommate noticed that Terri was gone and that she left the door wide open. Soon thereafter, I received a call that a young African American woman had taken her own life. It was Terri.

This is a horrendously tragic story. You may be wondering what it has to do with healing and self-care. I would say everything. As my grandmother would say, "It's the small foxes that destroy the vine."

Radical self-care is a life or death issue. The more we do it, the more we can tell we are worth showing up for, worth being cared for, worth speaking up for.

It's not Terri's fault that we live in a world that conditions women, particularly Black women and women of color, to believe that everyone's life is worth fighting for except theirs. It's not her fault that the combination of racism and sexism is so horrific that women and femmes—particularly Black, Brown and Indigenous women—have to sacrifice their own well-being to protect their men from the ravages of the criminal "justice" system. It's not her fault that we are told that we are here to provide comfort for the world. This story did not begin with Terri—it began with chattel slavery and the trauma memories that have been stored in our bodies and in our DNA—and this is why we need a radical process based in community. Radical self-care allows us a place to practice taking care of ourselves every day, little by little. It all adds up. We do not want what happened to Terri to continue to happen to other women and femmes.

I have sat with and listened to so many people talk about the isolation they feel and the internal conflict between their multiple and intersecting identities. We all know that the only winner of the "oppression Olympics" is the system that is designed to breed this kind of discord. That system has to collapse. We did not create the system, but it is our responsibility to dismantle it. And the only way that will happen is if you, I, and all of us take exquisite care of ourselves.

I remain hopeful as I encounter so many folks speaking up, getting real, and breaking their silence. I hold space with leaders from hundreds of organizations dedicated to all forms of liberation and social justice. They are working toward ending racism and male domination, fighting for immigrant rights, supporting mothers in times of crisis or the mental well-being of queer and trans youth, abolishing the prison industrial complex, and helping institutions confront their racist pasts.

All types of organizations and leaders are taking full days and sometimes longer to participate in healing retreats and workshops. Folks show up and bravely examine how they may have internalized the oppression, implementing some policies and practices that are in direct conflict with their commitment to social justice and liberation. People are getting free; sometimes in those spaces, right in the moment, I see people shed heavy trauma and grief. Something shifts when people tell their story and are listened to deeply by someone who can remember that they are amazing, awesome, and brilliant. You should know you are not alone, you can get free, it is not your fault, and you deserve support.

Consider engaging in one or a few of the OM remedies listed to help you remember that it is not your fault!

Get Free OM Remedies for Remembering It's Not Your Fault:

This OM remedy is really critical. It will be best if you can get a trusted friend or loved one, healer, or a professional therapist to be with you as you practice this OM remedy. This one is about crying, shaking, hollering, and getting the trauma up and out of your body.

- **Start with this mantra**: *I am really hurting and it's not my fault.* Each time you repeat it, allow your voice to get louder and louder until you are screaming. Seek the assistance of a professional counselor, healer, energy worker, bodyworker, or therapist. Do not try to address the effects of significant trauma by yourself.
- **Build a circle with a group of trusted friends**. Find trustworthy people with whom you can share your most painful experiences. Go ahead and allow yourself to get free, to tell those secrets in order to let go of the trauma, to allow yourself to fall apart. You are no longer that person who may have been alone and scared; you are powerful beyond measure.
- **Schedule a retreat** for your organization, your staff, and your leadership team with a focus on healing and radical self-care. You can also organize a retreat for you and your friends or family. Engage with a skilled and trusted facilitator of liberation, beyond yourself, so you can actually fully participate and get the support you need as well.

If you or someone you know is struggling with suicidal thoughts, it's critically important to get help. Contact your local suicide prevention hotline or, if you are in the US, do the following:

Call the National Suicide Prevention Lifeline at
1.800.273.8255
or
Text CONNECT to 741741 from anywhere in the USA

SEE ALSO:

BlackMentalHealthResources.net
TherapyForBlackGirls.com
LGBT National Hotline 1-888-843-4564
National Alliance on Mental Health: NAMI.org
PeoplesMovementCenter.com

#metoo I guess?

Dr. Joi Lewis

It's morning, y'all, and I am still mourning: senators, actors, fathers, brothers, preachers, friends, lovers, comrades, teachers, cousins, too many to name: men folks, toxic masculinity and its intersection with racism, heterosexism, and other forms of oppression and male domination.

I feel numb and I feel too much. Too much weight, too much worry, too much heartbreak. I feel lonely, like I wish I had company, but also I do not want to be bothered. The whole thing about sexual assault and violence against women. I feel in some ways like I cannot speak to it. I opted out.

I have been in a relationship with a woman for sixteen years. Somehow I thought maybe subconsciously that would protect me. In some ways I feel that as a "queer" identified person, I do not get to speak to this—that I will not be taken serious. I feel like I am invisible, that I don't have a right to speak, and that the many times I was groped, doors locked behind me, brushed up against too close, are simply things of the past.

#metoo, I guess?

But I am still asking Mother Spirit Ancestor Sojourner Truth's question: "Ain't I a woman?" She was born into slavery and gained her "freedom" in 1827. I was born "free" in 1969, and here we are in 2018, still confronted with many of the same realities.

I will keep reaching for my and your humanity. I will not swallow hate like it has been thrust upon our bodies, but I will not lay down and take it either. No jails can hold the amount of trauma we have endured.

First I am going to rest a bit, but not quit. #wegonebealright

Chapter 7

Let Your Heart Break Open

"I sat with my anger long enough, until she told me her real name was grief."
—Unknown

When I was growing up in East St. Louis in the '70s and '80s, people would often ask me why I always talked about my father and not my mother. My mother died of cancer when I was seven months old. I suspect her cancer came from ingesting the fumes emitted by the Monsanto chemical plant in the "town" (incorporated by Monsanto to avoid paying certain taxes) that bordered East St. Louis. When I told people of my mother's death, they always offered profuse apologies, and I always had the same reply: "It's okay, I didn't know her." That reply appeared to serve me well until fourteen years ago, when my niece, Dallas, was born. I spent a lot of time with her when she was an infant. I jumped at every chance possible to hold her close in my arms. One day, my sister needed to run some errands, so she left five-month-old Dallas with me. A few minutes after my sister left, my niece cried and cried and cried, nonstop. I could not find anything wrong with her: she was fed, she was dry, I was holding her . . . all seemed good. She wailed and wailed. I was so perplexed. As soon as my sister returned and Dallas heard her voice, the crying stopped.

From that day on I stopped saying that I did not know my mother. Dallas taught me that I did know her. I had grown inside her for nine months and lived with her for seven months after that. I realized how amazing it was for my mother to be with me even as she endured the pain of cancer. She was in so much pain that she could not hold me. We have no pictures of us together. Despite the pain, she named me Joi. Every time I hear my name, it is a gift from her and a reminder to hold the contradiction of simultaneous grief and joy. This requires that I let my heart break open.

The legacy of my relationship with my mother is a legacy of contradictions. As we live during this time of collective mourning, as we reach for our humanity, as we try to hold both joy and pain at the same time, we remember that joy and pain run from the same faucet.

I am reminded of this acutely right now. My dad passed away at the beginning of this past summer, and the ground shifted under my feet. When my mom passed away, my parents were twenty-eight years old. My sister was four and my brother was one. I cannot imagine what it was like for my dad, a young Black man, now a single father, who had to bury the love of his life. There was no therapy for his grief or ours. As I mourn his death and celebrate his life, I am conscious of the toll it took on him and on so many others to not get to talk about the pain, the grief, and the heartbreak. This shows up now in our reluctance to openly talk about heartbreak and how it affects our mental health. Mental health oppression and stigma are real.

Given all of what we are holding, depression will show up. I have held space for others—clients, friends, loved ones—during times of enormous grief, and I know many of the things to say and encourage people to do, but it is difficult to apply these to myself. This message is particularly for you, who normally hold it down for everyone else. You give out the hugs, burn the sage, massage the back, cook the food, give the rides, make the phone call, pay the bills, sing the song, write the poem, and clean up the mess.

This is for you: allow your heart to break. Let the tears come. Get help, go to the healing session, call the therapist.

Personally, I've been feeling like someone put a dimmer on what used to be a very bright light, but every time I try to adjust it, it won't work. I tell myself, "That's just how it is now," and that this is the new normal. Everything seems to be in slow motion, and it takes me triple the time to get things done. I am learning, and I offer this to you: little by slow, it gets better and a bit more bearable. The memories get more textured and at least offer some variety of joy and pain.

This week has been especially challenging. I have several deadlines I need to meet, including getting some revisions to my editor, recording some videos for my coaching clients, and closing out my dad's financial accounts. Closing out a bank account seems like it would be easy, but I realize the seemingly simple, mundane things can bring up lots of feelings and emotions. I closed the accounts and wrapped things up. I think having to do that one last thing was what was causing me to feel stuck. For my entire life and well before I was born, Dad did his banking at First Illinois Bank in East St. Louis, Illinois. So much of my dad's energy around money and providing for us, the family, and so many he cared about was connected to that bank. It symbolized a sense of community cultural wealth and social capital, yet his amazing work did not amass the wealth it deserved. I think there was something particularly heartbreaking about closing that chapter. Money and finances can bring up all kinds of stuff.

Money is energy, and it has to be thought about carefully. I now see how the energy of money tied up in my dad's connection to this institution was stirring up energy that was getting trapped in my body. I did not move as much as I would have liked to this week, and my food intake was okay, but not great.

However, instead of using this as an opportunity to be hard on myself, I used it as an opportunity to notice that I needed to let my heart break. I needed to pause, to be gentle with myself, to rest, and re-center. I needed to cry.

Perhaps you are in the midst of your own grief, some kind of loss, or some new reality. You may notice that you don't feel much like moving. Perhaps you are grabbing for more sugary or salty, crunchy things (my favorites). You might feel irritable and weepy. This is healing. Healing is such a beautiful word, and it can invoke feelings of calm and hope, but the process of healing can sometimes be painful, messy, and hard.

If you are feeling some kind of way, and your heart is aching, this is a good time to be gentle with yourself, pause, and take a minute.

It seems we are perpetually grieving for Black and Brown bodies gone too soon: Jamar Clark, Alton Sterling, Aiyana Jones, Mike Brown, Tamir Rice, Trayvon Martin, Oscar Grant, Sandra Bland, S'Sence Adams . . . the list goes on and on. How do we not collapse under the weight of what seems hopeless? Like so many before us, we find ways to reach for joy. As you reach for your humanity, and as I reach for mine, let us try to hold both joy and grief simultaneously. Let us remember that if we try to turn away and not face the pain and the grief, we also are turning off the joy. Grief and joy run from the same faucet.

Get Free OM Remedies for Letting Your Heart Break Open:

- **Notice contradictions:** When you feel grief or pain, look for the corresponding joy. When you feel hate, notice the people you love. When you feel rage, notice that you also have the capacity to feel compassion.
- **Cry every day:** Cry, even for a minute or two, every day. You can ask someone to listen to you without interrupting or offering advice, or simply cry by yourself. Cry hard. Allow the tears to flow freely down your face, and if it is available and allowable, get a really good cry out (you know, the "ugly cry," the kind where snot is running out of your nose and you can't find any tissue so you have to your sleeve or that of the trusted loved one that is with you). Consider setting a timer for a minute or two and letting yourself go ahead and cry hard until it goes off. The OM practice of crying and releasing the hold that grief and trauma can have on our bodies is so liberating.
- **Have a deep belly laugh:** Sometimes the way to allow your heart to break open is to allow it some joy. Laughing, even until you cry, is so good for you, and will give you a huge release. Make a "things that bring me joy" list: host a game night, dance to at least two of your favorite songs, make a date to hang with one of your favorite people, or watch a movie that really makes you happy, even if you have seen in one hundred times.

When the Tears Won't Stop
Dr. Joi Lewis

I just can't stop crying this morning.
I feel overcome with grief.
Grief is so rude, it never announces itself or makes an appointment.
It just barges in and interrupts your plans.

It's like the train that ran through my hometown in East St. Louis in
the mornings
right when we were trying to get school and my dad to work.
It would just make a full stop.
We would try to go around it and go over a few blocks,
but by the time we got there, it would be there blocking us again.

So we had to stop, wait, feel our frustrations.
There was no way around . . .
but eventually the train would start back up so we could cross the
tracks.

Well, that is what I am doing now.
I tried to go around, find other things to distract me
from the grief of losing my dad, but I could not seem to get around it.

As I sit here on the edge of my couch, in my meditation room,
surrounded by pictures of my loved ones, grandparents, my mom and
dad,

and my spiritual guide, each of their obituaries, they are now ancestors.

Tears are streaming down my face,
I do feel some release some surrender, maybe even some peace.

I am not yet on the other side of this grief,
I do not know if I ever will be,
but for now I am stopping and breathing and crying.

I am sure I look a mess and I feel like I am coming undone,
but what I know is that I am coming together, being more human.

This is emotional liberation, and I indeed am getting free.

If you keep trying to go around your feelings,
avoiding, looking for distractions,
consider stopping,
let the train start back when it does.
You will get there, but for now the most important place to be
is in your heart.

Chapter 8

Put on Your Own Mask First

"You are not required to set yourself on fire to keep other people warm."
—Unknown

This OM remedy may be challenging for you if, like me, you are often called on during times of tragedy to bring a healing presence to others. I needed a tool that would keep me from getting depleted every time I was called on and also a tool for knowing when to say no. When you have been taught your whole life to sacrifice yourself for your family and your community, you learn how to stuff your needs down and live with disappointment. In recent years, I have discovered a perfect visual: During a midair emergency on an airplane, oxygen masks fall from above the seats. Airlines always instruct you to put on your own mask before you try to assist others—even if you are traveling with a small child—because if something goes down and you do not have your mask on, you will not be able to assist anyone else. Same principle applies here, but unlike the airline, you must put on your metaphorical mask way before take-off, before the flight is even booked. You have to anticipate what is coming. I learned this lesson the hard way.

When I was offered a position as a dean of students at a small college in California, I was asked to move there from Minnesota in less than a month so that I could begin before the students arrived. I knew it was a big job and that I would get called on for all kinds of emergency situations. I knew I needed time to put on my own mask first. So I agreed to move but insisted on not starting until I had at least two weeks to get settled, to get grounded and get my bearings. Travel there was a huge challenge. The plane was delayed because of bad weather, and when we arrived, half of our luggage was lost. I wanted to get to campus, get the keys, and then rest.

As dean of students, I was required to live on campus. The house I was to live in was not yet ready, so I went to pick up the keys to my temporary apartment. When I walked into the president's office, I could sense that something was wrong, but no one said anything. After arriving in the temporary apartment, I received a call from one of the associate deans. She did not sound good. "Dr. Joi, I know you have not started work yet," she said, "but you are the only dean we have, and we need help." When I asked what was happening, she said, "One of our students has been murdered." She reported that no one else was injured. It actually happened on a college campus on the East Coast while the student was home for the summer visiting family. Her high school boyfriend brutally murdered her, and at the time the only clue they had of who she might be was her college ID in the back pocket of her jeans.

In a matter of minutes, I became the spokesperson for the institution. I had to talk to the media, the family, and other students. I was somewhat in shock yet had no time to notice. I did not know what to do. I had never been a dean of students before. My plan had been to ease into getting there and then learn how to get around. I did what many of us do when we are in charge in a time of crisis. I stuffed down my feelings, pushed through my fatigue, and covered up my own grief. I had to show up for others.

We did get through it, and I was appreciated for showing up and dealing with such a difficult situation. All of my martyr tendencies were validated, but my being a martyr affected not only me but also my staff; I was worn out, and they were too. Although I realize it was good that I was so available and responsive during that significant time of need, I paid a high price for not listening to my gut, for not insisting that I start two weeks later, which would have allowed me the time I needed to put on my own mask first. It took me well over a year to recover from that, but it inspired me to create a tool enabling me to put on my own mask in advance.

Given the amount of trauma generated by state-sponsored violence and inhumane practices, you as a facilitator of liberation will be constantly called upon to respond and react. Unfortunately, these continued traumatic events are not surprising. However, as a matter of course, the response is often surprise. We so want to believe that we won't keep waking up to these tragedies. We have made our request very clear: "Stop killing us," "Stop raping us," and "Stop breaking up our families."

Although I believe that we will win, I want us to be alive and well when that happens. This requires us to take care of ourselves and to demand that resources be put in place to build real infrastructures that support long-term healing in community. It is expected that those of us who care deeply about issues of justice will continue to do the heavy lifting—mostly unpaid, invisible emotional labor. It's even more important that we practice radical self-care as a form of putting on our own masks first, not just in the moment of the emergency but all the time. We cannot be Uber for healing. There should be a crisis response, but we should not be building a crisis response structure in the moment; we must build it in advance so that we can respond from a place of abundance.

I learned that I needed not so much to manage my time as my energy. I began to think about my emotional energy like a bank account.

We know how much money we have in the bank, and we need to be just as clear about how much energy we have in our emotional bank. This will help us to put on our own mask first. I realized that I had way more withdrawals than I had deposits. I was writing a lot of bad checks.

In moments of stress, our instinct is to react with the old patterns of neural wiring in the brain (i.e., our conditioning)—whatever way we learned to deal with stress in the first eighteen months of our lives, which likely continued during childhood and our early twenties. The good news is that the brain never stops learning. It has the ability to lay down new wiring and grow new cells up until we die. This is called *neuroplasticity*, and it is very, very good that we have this. Neuroplasticity allows the nerve cells in the brain to compensate for injury and disease and to adjust their activities in response to new situations or to changes in their environment. It means that despite the traumas of our early childhood and after, we can rewire our brain to respond differently—more skillfully, more resiliently—in the present. When we get the things that are bothering us up and out, they lose their hold on us. It's both spiritual and scientific. We can literally rewire our brain and thus our body's response to past and present trauma. This is filling up our energy bank with healthy deposits.

Every time you meditate, sing, dance, cry, tell your story, get that trauma out, or create a more liberated way to respond in the present moment to the past trauma, you change the game. When you tell your story of trauma and get help, you switch up your response. Now this memory of healing will interrupt some of those earlier memories of trauma. Reorganizing your brain in this way requires intentionally thinking about and doing things differently than you used to, which includes putting your own mask on first.

Get Free OM Remedies for Putting on Your Own Mask First:

- **Create your "energy" bank account:** Decide which people, places, and things are deposits and withdrawals from your energy account. It is okay for there to be withdrawals, but you have to make sure you have enough in your account that you are not bouncing checks. Create a list of deposits (things and people that fill you up, such as music, friends, exercising, meditation, dancing). Also create a list of withdrawals—things that take your energy (talking to toxic people, paying bills, cleaning the house, sitting in traffic). Before you withdraw, always make sure that you've already deposited enough.
- **Get a massage or a loving hug** from a trusted loved one or some bodywork. Healthy touch stimulates production of the hormone oxytocin. This is the antidote to cortisol, and it helps us settle down in times of crisis or when we're feeling antsy. You can use hugs (long ones, at least twenty seconds) and other physical touch—including your own—to quickly raise your oxytocin when you need it.
- **Join a collective of healers or facilitators of liberation:** Connect with other space holders and cultural healers, and learn how to monetize your emotional labor so that you are able to do this work in a humane and sustainable way. Do not agree to always show up during crisis when some preparation and resources can be made available in advance. Join a community of healers through the Find Calm in Chaos course: https://joiunlimited. com/calm-in-chaos/.

Practice 4

Conscious Movement

(Get Going)

Chapter 9

Answer the Door!

"Give light and people will find the way."
—Ella Baker

I have been doing this work now for over twenty-five years. I now know it is healing work, and it helps me hold contradictions, find calm in chaos, find the joy in the pain, find healing in the heartbreak. I have seen a lot of heartbreak, and I know you have too. Through doing this work and spending countless hours in rooms in healing circles with you and so many others, I keep hearing from many of you that you feel defeated. Although you may not be ready to give up on life, fighting for justice, shifting policy, or transforming communities, you have considered it. It feels like it would be easier to give up.

I get it. You may often be willing to do whatever it may take to make an impact on the world but sometimes have trouble actually getting up. You might literally get stuck in the bed, on the couch, or in front of the TV. This is so real. I hear this loud and clear. I have been there— not just in some distant past, but last week. But then it happens: I see evidence of the universe conspiring for my most benevolent outcome.

One day, I was minding my own business and taking one of those good summer naps. I really wanted to get some space from the world and isolate myself—which is sometimes disguised as "self-care"—but I knew better. I was in my bed in a deep sleep in the house my partner and I had purchased about a year before. We'd moved from a fancy neighborhood in St. Paul, right around the corner from the governor's mansion, to the Frogtown neighborhood, which is one of the most diverse neighborhoods in Minnesota and has a deep and rich history and an amazing community garden. That said, there is also a lot of struggle and a lot of heartbreak here, things that can come with life in an under-resourced area. We moved there for all of these reasons. We wanted to live where lots of youth of color lived, particularly young Black people. We wanted to build deep connections with them and their families, so we moved here to Frogtown, a neighborhood much like the one where I grew up in East St. Louis.

I wanted to build these relationships but hadn't yet done so. On the day of my long summer nap, my big break happened. Three young Black boys were fighting across the street from our house and using a bunch of four-letter words. I went outside, broke up the fight, and held court, telling them that they were kings and descendants of kings and did not get to treat each other that way. In about ten minutes, they returned to the innocence that eight-year-olds get to have. They came back to our house almost every day that summer, and they brought others. They come to meditate, make oils and scrubs, tumble on the mats, and eat popsicles.

I was often moved by my connection with them and by their ability to be such amazing teachers and mentors to me. They got me to show up for my daily practice of the Orange Method: meditating and getting grounded, getting mindful and being fully in the present moment, letting my heart break and getting some emotional liberation, and getting out of the house and consciously moving.

Here's another story: Last year, a few of the boys came over. They wanted popsicles, but first we had to discuss them stealing my bike pump. We worked it out, though they were some tough little boys. As we were talking, up walked two little girls whom I never met before. They were both seven and just as tough as the boys. And they were beautiful. I sent the boys away to work off their debt for my bike pump and earn their popsicles, and I started talking to the little girls. I asked them questions: What are your names? How old are you? What is your favorite subject in school? One said, "Mnes is ballet."

"Awesome," I replied. "I want to make sure everyone can hear you loud and clear, so let's repeat that but drop the s, and say 'Mine is ballet.'" With big smiles, the girls repeated after me: Mine is ballet. I asked the girls if they knew the name of the famous Black ballerina. They did not and asked me, their eyes wide with anticipation, "What's her name?" I wracked my brain, but Misty Copeland's name wouldn't come to me. As they left, I promised them I'd figure it out—and held out the possibility that someday everyone would know *these girls'* names.

I returned to the house to get popsicles for the boys, and when I came back out, about twenty young people were on the corner fighting hard. It was a mess. I jumped into it to pull one big boy off a younger boy. It was intense, and things were heated. I managed to break up the fight. I took a minute to catch my breath, and then I felt a tug on my shirt. It was one of the girls. She had found a picture of Misty Copeland. "Dr. Joi, look," she said, pointing to a cell phone in her hand. "Is this her?" This feisty young girl busted through a heated fight to show me this. With this determined act, she gave me life. She reminded me to stay focused, no matter what.

Healing is designed to get us out of isolation, out of our heads, out of our homes, out of shame and hopelessness, and stay focused on what really matters—just as the neighborhood kids inspired me to do. The young people in my neighborhood are a constant reminder that building community is not convenient. Since that fight, now three summers ago, a regular crew of young people often come to our home, which is now a kind of secondary community center for them. They knock on the front door, and if we do not answer, they knock on all of the doors or windows until we answer. They usually do not want much, mostly to be connected. Popsicles are a bonus.

You may read this and think that they are lucky to have us, but I would say we are luckier for having them. On so many days, they have saved me from isolation, from despair, from being self-absorbed. It's still a practice, and I don't always enthusiastically answer the door—literally or metaphorically. It's okay to rest and have some downtime, but the more we are connected and engaged, it becomes easier to distinguish between downtime and isolation.

After you're done reading this book, I want you to be able to open the door, break up the fights, hold heartbreak, and look oppression dead in the face—both the kind that comes at us and the kind we internalize.

Radical self-care is not about saving the world; it's about reclaiming our humanity in community.

Get Going OM Remedies for Answering the Door

- **Answer the door!** The main remedy here is to do whatever it takes to get out of isolation. When someone else takes the initiative in your direction and knocks on your door, answer it! Respond to that text or answer the phone.

- **Knock on someone else's door.** Take some initiative in some-one else's direction. Invite yourself over to someone else's house, or invite them to yours. Text or call someone just to let them know you're thinking about them.
- **Get out and play.** Spend time in your neighborhood, go out and listen to some live music, attend a play, or take a walk and strike up a conversation with someone else who is walking in the same direction you are. (This may require putting away the cell phone.)

Open Heart

Dr. Joi Lewis

May my heartbreak be heard like a song

May my body be an offering that gives back so much of what has been poured into it

May cleaning out the refrigerator be a mediation, not a chore

May it be a time to remember abundance

May brushing my teeth count as conscious movement, with extra points for flossing

May lotion be my essential oil to smooth out the rough places

May walking to my car in the snow count as exercise,

and pushing away from the table count as a push-up

May getting out of bed be the opening ceremony to small practices of radical self-care.

Let it all count: the emoji-answered text, the extra minute in the shower, the holding of my tongue, the bowing of my head, the turning off the TV, the eating one tomato, the picking up the phone.

May it be celebrated like a graduation, a wedding, a promotion. For every time we show up for ourselves, it is indeed a miracle.

Chapter 10

Recruit a Radical Self-Care Squad

"When you want to go fast, go alone. When you want to go far, go together."
—African Proverb

If you already have a squad or a special group of friends, that's awesome. I want you to recruit a #RadicalSelfCareSquad. My rule is to always go at least two by two. You need company—someone to have your back, a shoulder to lean on, and someone who will remember that you are amazing, awesome, and brilliant. Sure, you can do things by yourself, but it's much better with company. Talk to anyone who has been to my workshops or retreats, and you'll learn that I almost always want to find a way to quickly help people build a sense of belonging, to make the room smaller, and to get connected. I facilitate some kind of team-building exercise that allows participants to talk to several people, and eventually each is paired with someone who becomes a "high-five buddy." Later, high-five buddies connect with one or two other pairs, and you form a squad. This is critically important at a workshop or retreat when the focus is on healing and radical self-care—particularly as we begin to unpack issues of oppression and liberation. If you need a buddy and squad in a workshop or retreat, you definitely need one in real life.

I am fond of calling everyone my cousins, which is huge because, when I was growing up, there was no higher honor than to have cousins. I like to think we are all cousins. Your cousins are not limited to those who have the same blood running through their veins or even folks who look like you. We have close cousins and distant cousins, but they are all cousins nonetheless and are our fictive kin.

When my grandmother, Ms. Trudy B. Lewis, passed away in 1992, she had thirty-three grandchildren and forty-four great-grandchildren. Each of us claimed that we were her favorite. (I really was her favorite, but I let the others think that they were.) My grandmother had a fourth-grade education but a PhD in wisdom. She taught my cousins and me how to have each other's back, how to work through conflict, and how to make up quickly. These lessons have literally saved my life.

In the humid summers of East St. Louis, my cousins made the hundred-degree heat not just bearable but fun. We played four-square, jacks, and volleyball over the clothesline in Grandmama's backyard. Thanks to our big cousin Kei Kei, at seven and eight years old we learned how to roller skate in the middle of the street and avoid traffic and how to go on three-hour bike rides and time our stop at Church's Chicken for a courtesy cup of ice. Kei Kei let us skateboard through the academic buildings while she was in class because they had the best ramps inside, and because of this we learned that we belonged on a college campus. We learned how to be rule-breakers and stick together. If one person was caught, we were all going to take the fall.

Now I don't live anywhere near the cousins I grew up with. But after growing up in East St. Louis, I've learned how to claim almost everybody as my cousin. My cousins and I did not always see eye to eye—for example, they did not want to accept that I was my grand-mother's favorite—but they taught me that life is more fun with company. My cousins were my first squad, and I learned that you need a squad to make this journey work.

I live my life as a transplant in Minnesota and travel all over the country and the world, but I try to find my cousins everywhere I go. You can be my cousin too. I moved away from home twenty-five years ago, and I have been a part of amazing communities along the way: my sorority sisters at Southern Illinois University at Edwardsville, Iowa State University, and the University of Minnesota; "The Cousins," my Black Colleagues at Macalester College; sista circles in Minnesota and Oakland; My cousins from the Givens Foundation Writing Fellowship; and my OMies from my coaching fellowship.

I have had many squads over the years, yet there have been gaps in time that left me feeling lonely and isolated. I have learned that you really need to keep at least one squad going at all times. The process of radical self-care is not one you can truly practice alone. You need your people. I know life can be a lot, but you do not have to do it alone.

You need folks in your squad who are going to track you,
check in on you, pick up the phone, or even drive to your house
if they have not heard from you.

When I started writing this book, I noticed I kept getting stuck, not only related to the book but with life. It was getting hard for me to show up for myself every day. I was spending a lot of time in bed, often working but unable to get up and do life. My vision for do-ing work with emotional laborer (healers, social justice advocates, helping professionals and senior leaders) had become clearer and bigger. That was both exciting and at times daunting, so my self-doubt often snuck in.

The more I thought about and talked about radical self-care as my mission, the harder it became for me to do it in my own life. Even though I knew at the core of my being how important it is to have my people, my cousins in this journey, those limiting beliefs rose up. I realized I needed to remember and experience again how difficult it was to try to do things by myself and to be on my own. My grandmother always said, "Many hands make light work." So, once again, I needed to find my cousins to get a squad.

I felt somewhat uncomfortable asking for help. I didn't want to bother anyone, as everyone was so busy. I could not ask anyone to give me some time, blah, blah, blah. However, I had to admit to myself that I was struggling. We all sometimes need help getting off the struggle bus. Sometimes we need to know that someone will be there to meet us and offer a soft place to land where we won't be judged and can be fully ourselves—the not-so-cleaned-up version of ourselves—and still get welcomed and affirmed.

I had joined many groups over the years, but I was also an expert at being alone with a roomful of people. Now I had to step out on faith and get the courage and the humility to ask for help so I could practice what I was preaching, or in this case, what I was writing. I had to squad up, and I invite you to do the same.

OM Remedy Activity

I reached out to five friends to join my #RadicalSelfCareSquad, #TeamJoi, for ninety days. I asked if they would each give me fifteen minutes once a week, one hour a month, for a total of three hours over a three-month period. Each friend was my "accountability partner" on a different weekday. I called that person in the morning, usually by eight thirty, and had a check-in about my life.

We usually practiced some version of the Orange Method:

1. We meditated or got grounded for about two minutes.
2. I practiced getting present and mindful about the day. I shared my intentions and commitments for being aware (e.g., being mindful with my food, not only what I was eating but where and how).
3. I tried to be vulnerable and share some emotional liberation. I shared something that was bothering me or something I wrote in my journal that morning. I tried to let the emotion come and not pretend that I was okay.
4. I shared my commitment to some conscious movement, moving my body in some way (yoga, dancing, running, going for a walk, parking farther from the entrance when I was running errands), which helped me both physically and emotionally.

These short phone calls turned into a precious and sacred time. What was originally fifteen minutes for me turned into at least a half hour for each of us. We cheered each other on, provided a shoulder to cry on when needed, and enjoyed belly laughs together. We were that loud voice that drowned out the others that said we couldn't do these things: write that book, make it as an entrepreneur, or carve out time for yoga, therapy, or a trip away.

You are not limited only to people who look like you, whose lives are similar to yours, or who are already in your life. Do not limit yourself. My #RadicalSelfCareSquad peeps are straight, queer, Muslim, Christian, white, Black, South Asian, women, gender non-conforming, full-time workers, entrepreneurs, nonprofit execs, Southerners, Midwesterners, and international.

I am with one of my squad members today. We have known each other for twenty-five years. Until she agreed to join my squad, we had not talked on the phone for more than three times. We were Facebook friends and kept up that way. But this year, we spent a week together supporting each other to write our books and live our biggest lives as entrepreneurs.

Yes, you need your cousins, your squad far and wide.

Get Going OM Remedies for Creating a Radical Self-Care Squad:

OM Remedy Practice: Create a #RadicalSelfCareSquad

- **Remember that it is okay to ask for help.** Someone is likely waiting for the opportunity to connect with you.
- **Make a list of people** you love and who you know love you who would be great to connect with once a week. Don't limit your list to only folks you are connected to now on a regular basis, but think about that friend or loved one you have not talked to in a long time but whom you deeply love and who cares for you. Write her or his name down and add it to your list.
- **Text, email, or call your people.** Below is a sample note I sent. You can edit with your story and go squad up.

Sample email or text:

Hey, it's (put your name here) . . .

Let me warn you—this is a super long note. But I wanted to send it to you before I gave you a call, which I hope to do in the next few minutes. I know we have not been in touch recently, but I know we are still connected. Please respond and let me know if you are interested. First of all, I hope you are well. I am reaching out to you now because I love you, and I know you love me. I am putting together a radical self-care squad, #TeamJoi, as I go forward after my full health and well-being. I would love for you to be on it.

I am committed to my own radical self-care so that I can also hold space for others. My ask is that you commit to listening to me and praying with me for fifteen minutes once a week. It would be the same day and time every week, God willing. I am asking for a three-month commitment. I will send you an invitation with possible times.

That is a total of fifteen minutes a week, one hour a month, and three hours over three months—with also being "on call" once a week, so definitely no more than a six total-hour commitment over the next three months.

I would like to start on Monday, February 19. The times would be scheduled sometime 6–8:30 a.m. CST. I will send a calendar invite, and you choose the times that work best for you. I will confirm your time by Sunday no later than 4:00 p.m. I would call you during our designated time.

I am planning on having these calls with different people five days a week. If possible, I would like to end the three-month period with a video call with the entire #TeamJoi on Saturday, May 19, likely at 10 am CST.

Why do I need this? I realize that I have huge isolation patterns, but I am very high functioning. When I am going about my daily life, I can easily fall into patterns that do not serve me. Those patterns may be eating unhealthy food, isolating myself, not moving my body, overworking, or working in the bed. Generally, I am not interacting with people. I want to work on these things with company. Also, I am asking you to bear witness to remind me of my commitments and not to collude with me. I know that I am called to do the work of holding space for radical self-care and healing for women, especially for Black women, women of color, and femmes who have struggled with their weight, but I have to get the support I need. I am the largest I have been in the last six years since moving back to Minnesota, and my blood pressure is super high. At the same time, my business is booming and growing, and I want to really live fully. So I need to connect daily with someone who loves me and who can be a mirror to me as I go after God's plan for me. I do understand if you cannot commit, but it's so good for me to reach out.

I still want to be in your life and talk with you about your life and all things that are going on with you—but for these fifteen minutes it is important for it to be "my time."

Basically, I would like to practice the Orange Method every day for the next three months.

1. Mediation (get grounded)
2. Mindfulness (get present)
3. eMotional Liberation (get free)
4. Conscious Movement (get up, get going)

These four practices would guide our calls, and I have goals in each area.

Month 1:

1. Meditate for at least ten minutes daily.
2. Be mindful of what I put in my body (no white flour or refined sugar for the first month). Also to write down my commitments for food, work, and connections.

3. Write, cry, express my feelings about my life to another human being during my daily call, and journal for at least ten minutes a day.
4. Move my body for at least thirty minutes a day, five days a week.

Much love,

Joi

Chapter 11

Get off the Struggle Bus

"It is never easy to demand the most of ourselves, from our
lives, from our work.
To encourage excellence is to go beyond the encouraged
mediocrity of our society
is to encourage excellence."
—Audre Lorde

To live in this complicated world, you have to learn to time travel, to dream your way into a new reality, and to imagine what may be possible beyond what you can see in front of you. How can you get there? Let's start by acknowledging that the "struggle bus" is not reliable transportation to a new reality. In fact, the struggle bus will keep taking you on the same route, where all of the street signs have limiting beliefs. It will keep you in self-doubt and insecurity. The struggle bus will have you bumping around in the hills of settling, denying yourself love, staying in a job or career that does not feed your soul, or living a much smaller life than you were meant to. You know you're on it when the things you want to change aren't changing, when you can't stop complaining about your life and telling everyone how miserable you are, or when you have no perspective or sense of possibility. It does not have to be this way.

I was on the struggle bus for several years. I had a twenty-plus-year career on college campuses as dean and vice president, and I enjoyed many of those years. But something deep down in my belly knew that I wanted to work beyond the walls of the ivory tower. I wanted to be my own boss, but I was too intimidated to make that kind of move. I had an opportunity after finishing my doctorate work to go that route, but I was too scared.

I bought into the idea that if I worked
really hard, long hours and weekends, took emergency calls
at night, tried to be everything to everybody, and ignored my
own needs, I would get what the system promised.

For many of these years, I used food to numb the fatigue, the stress, and the heartbreak of working in higher education. At the same time, I was worrying about various family members who were struggling under the relentless weight of racism, classism, and sexism. I believed that if I kept going as I had been, I would benefit from a secure pathway to my dream job as a college president. I was kind of living the life in Northern California, as a dean of students and vice provost at a small women's college.

I knew that I did not want to stay on the struggle bus, so I took the upgrade. For five years, I was off the struggle bus and on the "promise plane." I committed to a practice of radical self-care, lost 120 pounds, and started practicing meditation, mindfulness, and yoga. I had daily contact with people who offered me real support and understanding. I thought I had finally exited the struggle bus forever.

When I left Oakland and moved back to Minnesota, where I took a job as a vice president and chief diversity officer at a large community college, I got right back on the struggle bus. I wanted so much to believe that if I stayed the course, the struggle bus would eventually take a detour and get me to where I was really making a difference in the lives of students I cared about deeply. I still thought that, one day, I would become a college president, but that never happened. Instead, I stayed on the struggle bus and endured levels of racism beyond my comprehension.

I dealt with a lot of stress and regret, and my commitment to radical self-care began to slip. I gained back most of the weight I had lost, and I quit my job after only nine months. I was still doing my inside work of healing and meditation, but it was no match in that moment for the weight of the systemic oppression I was feeling. For a time, I went to my bed and pulled the covers over my face. Days became weeks, and weeks became months, and I stayed in deep despair. I did not know what to do.

Fortunately, at that low point I decided again to work to be done with the struggle bus. I'm not entirely done yet, though I'm on my way. The bus rolls by some days, and it does slow down long enough so I could get on. I am tempted, but I let it keep going. After I quit my job, I signed up for a yoga teachers' training class. I became a certified yoga teacher and began a yearlong commitment to my own radical self-care. I meditated and practiced mindfulness. I prayed, cried, and started putting myself out there.

My grandmother used to say that you have to "separate your who from your do." I used to be very fond of saying that I was fortunate enough to have jobs that allowed me to do my work, but that I would do my work even if I did not have a job. That was real cute when I had a job, but when I quit my job, I had to revisit that question and determine if I was still going to really do my work. I decided that I would.

I launched my coaching and consulting firm, Joi Unlimited. I realized that all of those experiences I had from growing up in East St. Louis, plus working for over twenty years on college campuses and living life, prepared me to do the work of social justice and healing in the world.

At first, I did not know how to really start or run a business. I did not know what to charge, so I undercharged and left hundreds of thousands of dollars on the table. I tried to offer a lot and meet every possible need. I wrote grants and worked myself to exhaustion. But through a combination of trial and error and working with some mentors along the way, I shifted things. I now run a very successful coaching and consulting business. I have surpassed financially what I was making working on a college campus, and more importantly, I am able to make a more direct impact on the communities and people I care about most.

If you are still on the struggle bus now, know there is another way. If you are trying to decide whether you can take a leap of faith and you want to figure out how to monetize your life experience—your expertise as a social justice advocate, healer, or helper—you can do it. Get yourself a mentor and coach, and get off the struggle bus.

Get Going OM Remedies for Getting off the Struggle Bus

- Write down your biggest fear about taking the leap.
- Write down what you really wish you could do every day for work.
- Write down what is standing in the way of your own radical self-care.
- Write down what you think you need from a mentor to help you create a transition plan to get you to a life you really want and to get off the struggle bus for good.

It Came Back

Dr. Joi Lewis

It came back!

That's the thing—I am not exactly sure when.

One day it fit neatly in the whole of the closet,

I did not even have to check before I jumped into the shower,

Just pull something off the shelf, and it would always work just fine.

What year did it come back?

I am not sure . . .

Sometime between 2009 when they shot Oscar Grant at the BART station in Oakland and the McKinney pool party fiasco in Texas summer of 2015.

I woke up, and it came back, nearly all of it.

I think it was trying to make room for heartbreak and joy all at once.

It was trying to hold at least three hospital stays for Dad,

a three-day adventure at Disneyland with my seven-year-old niece,

three moves, one from California to Minnesota in 2007;

a move back to Minnesota in April of 2012

where I finally could be close to my niece and sister again;

then another move from Minnesota to E. St. Louis that same year in August.

This time my sister and niece made the move.

So much happened between those years.

I got a new job and was well on my way to becoming a college president,

then nine months later it was gone.

It's as if it never left, maybe it never left really,

and I dreamed the whole thing

But then how did I end up with a closet full of size 8 pants that I used to just pull right up

And now I can barely get one leg in—70 pounds of the 120 pounds I lost found me

in places I wanted to forget about.

Perhaps it found me so I won't lose it this time

but rather feel the feelings and

really release my fear of going to those places

of deep grief and sadness I packed away.

When I realized I can indeed hold contradictions, the heartbreak and joy

When my childhood just up and left me.

Chapter 12

Live Your Best Life

"The revolution will be healing."
—Chani Nicholas, healer, astrologer, writer

Dear one,

Thank you so much for going on this journey with me. I hope that you found some comfort between these pages and took some time to be in your body a bit more, connect with some old friends, try something new, and let go of some things that no longer serve you—or, at least, temporarily put them down. You may have noticed this is not a book of answers, and it may have actually raised more questions. My biggest hope is that you can now remember that you are amazing, awesome, and brilliant.

A lot has shifted for me since I started this book project. At the beginning, I kept getting in my own way. I kept trying to figure out why my higher power, who I call God, decided that my work would be grounded in the practices of healing and radical self-care. Why couldn't I have been given a different calling, something that I am actually really good at? Like sleeping in, pulling the covers over my head, and not wanting to get up; eating cake and hot chips and managing to leave vegetables on my plate uneaten; not exercising for weeks; or skipping flossing sometimes (well, okay, a lot).

I was sure if evaluated, I would be in the expert category of any of these, especially if we broke it down by age group. Why is my calling not something that I am good at? I kept asking that question over and over. Instead of choosing one of the four things I listed above to dedicate my life to, I decided to stop resisting and just surrender. I realized that surrender does not mean defeat. I accepted my calling and embraced the struggle to feel my feelings, to reveal at least some of my secrets, and to rest but not quit. I am dedicated to making an Olympic sport out of healing and radical self-care. You have to practice it often and spend lots of time on it.

Radical self-care has been a struggle for me, but with practice I am getting so much better at it, and I will keep repeatedly showing up for it. I decided once and for all that I was not going to give up, and like those Olympic stars, I am continually practicing, putting in hundreds of hours.

I have the scrapes, scars, wounds, and bandages to prove it. I wanted to be able to write my story and have the before-and-after pictures. I have pictures of me overweight, wearing clothes that are not flattering, but still having a kind of smile. Then there are the "after" pictures from when I lost 120 pounds. But I have even more pictures of me gaining most of those pounds back four years later and still holding on to them for almost four more years. (Thank you, universe, for revealing to me that gaining weight very quickly and holding on to it is a special skill of mine.) There is not and never will be an "after" picture, and today I can say I am thankful for that. I get to be in it, and I hope you will stay in it with me and the rest of the OMies as we travel with all of our cousins.

This process has taught me some important lessons and given me some beautiful gifts. Here is what is true: what was before is now in the past, and "after" is in some made-up future time that may never come. All we really have is right now, the present moment.

The radical self-care I subscribe to and promote is less about goals like trips to the gym, time at the spa, eating vegetables, and drinking water. It is about dreaming with my eyes wide open. It's about running fast, jumping high, getting to yell, raising hell, eating cake, and drinking libations early in the morning. It's about loving me now, not the me I hope to be or the "we" I hope we become. It's about knowing we are alright now. I understand that the system is set up so that we do not take care of ourselves, particularly us Black people. The system wants us tired, broken, isolated, sick, and disconnected, and we will collude with the system and commit harmful acts to ourselves and to others. We will both internalize oppression and run our oppression patterns on others.

I have a great deal of experience with radical self-care as a process, not as a destination. I have seen what happens and how our lives change and shift when I show up for this practice on a daily basis and when I encourage others to do the same.

Healing is not about getting to a destination or about feeling good in the moment. It is about getting free, showing up, asking for help, and talking about those places where you are not sure if you want to continue. It's about the exposing the hidden path that makes you turn in on yourself. Like this week, when I could not stop eating foods that keep me in low vibrations: pizza, donuts, cookies, potato chips. I don't even know how the food really tasted because I was not eating it for the taste. I was to try to plug up a God-size hole. I wanted it to fill up the grief of losing my dad, the kids who knocked on my door and said they were hungry, my sister-friend who is fighting to keep her kids but can barely feed herself, and hearing that another trans Black woman was murdered.

This is my attempt to say something about the world we are living in. Cruelty is awful. It's all awful that children being taken away from their parents at the borders, in the "hood," and on the reservation. Of course you and I are affected; we are human. Don't stop reaching for your humanity or mine, even if it might be in between reaching for potato chips. Healing sometimes hurts, because it requires slowing down long enough to consider that food, drugs, sex, shopping, and gambling won't heal us. Noticing what we really feel, and that we are connected to others, will.

Healing is about embracing the heartbreak and joy, and heartbreak and joy, and heartbreak and joy.

It's talking about the isolation you feel when you're in a room full of people. It's about exposing the lies you have been told about there being something wrong with you that you need to be ashamed of. It's the way mental health challenges show up. It's about calling out a world that has been organized to crush your spirit and calling up the universe and the divine that has been set up for our greater good. It's demanding that we get to have our minds, our spirits, our families, and our communities. It's exposing lies and claiming our liberation. What is true about who you are is that you are amazing, awesome, and brilliant. You are not damaged or defective. Something awful happened to you, and to your people: genocide, chattel slavery, internment camps, or concentration camps. Then it was declared to be "over," by some law, by some man, but it never stopped. You were supposed to just "recover," move on, make nice, and be thankful. Healing is about acknowledging this, and affirming that you did not make it up. It's also true that you come from ancestors who love you, who love the earth and every living thing. You are magic and meaning.

They tried to bury us, but they
did not know that we were seeds.
—Mexican Proverb

Radical self-care allows us to live our best life and makes it possible to be in more than one place at a time. It's kind of like time traveling, but not exactly. I keep having this experience more and more, ever since I took the leap and manifested what I wanted. I began to believe I could have a big life, and I took the action steps to make it happen. No, I didn't sprinkle stardust in my eyes (although I am not opposed to that). I am just letting my heart break wide open and realizing that is healing, and it allows me to hold both joy and pain.

For instance, holidays can be super complicated and bring up all kind of trauma. For a variety of reasons, including some grounded in oppression, my partner and I do not always spend the holidays together. This used to be a source of tension. This healing and radical self-care journey gave me the ability to spend Thanksgiving week with my family in East St. Louis and also be with my partner in Florida with her folks. I know what you are thinking: that is not possible. But indeed it happened. This is the magic of healing. When in East St. Louis, I was fully present with no regrets, and I also was very much alive in my sweetie's heart.

Healing and radical self-care give you the space and encouragement to fight for, grieve over, and seek out a kind of love that reaches for each other's humanity. I have witnessed the love and power that healing and radical self-care cultivate, not only in intimate partner relationships but also between seemingly disparate groups and between people who were never meant to be in the same room with each other. It's almost never easy to hang in there through someone's well-deserved anger about racism and its intersection with other forms of oppression, although I have seen people stick with it in very intense rooms.

Much like the phrase "radical self-care," when you hear "healing," images of serenity and peace may come to mind. However, before you get to the peace and calm, you often have to take a hard look at the pain, hurt, disappointment, devastation, heartbreak, and collapse that oppression and trauma have produced. As a participant in one of the recent healing retreats I led shared, "This healing is not a kumbaya moment." It can sometimes be super intense, with yelling, crying, shaking, and cursing mixed in with laughter, dancing, yoga, hugging, and listening. It requires time for long and deep discussions, heated arguments, compromise, sometimes settling, and the dogged belief that we are worth fighting for.

Healing and radical self-care make space for grace, laughter,
moments to cry and feel disappointment, and sometimes
dissatisfaction.

Radical self-care does not require me to go small or be isolated or give up my family, my culture, my race, my people, my dreams, or my faith—it makes it all much more possible.

Healing helps you to face the deep sense of loss you may feel when you are away from your loved ones or you consider the pain and suffering your ancestors endured or inflicted. When I am in Minnesota, I miss waking up to the sounds of my brother making breakfast for my dad before he passed away and the anticipation of my sister and my niece coming over. I miss my dad hollering my name through the house with extreme urgency only to learn that he would like me to add some more essential oil to the new diffuser I bought for him, even though the bottle is right by his bed. I miss driving ten minutes to drop in and see my aunties and cousins just because I can. However, I am not sad—because these times remind me of how expansive love is. Love can hold heartbreak and healing all at once. I am truly grateful for this journey called life and that I can be in more than one place at a time.

I will be fully living life in St. Paul, or whatever part of the world this wonderful life takes me, but I am comforted by knowing I will also still get to be in my happy place in East St. Louis, snuggled in bed in my childhood bedroom with those same pink walls and floral drapes, and, more importantly, be in the hearts and minds of my loved ones there. Love is indeed big enough. Please know this love of which I speak is not reserved for only me; it is available to us all. Our ancestors teach us how to be in many places all at once. Every day and every time we think of our grandmother's sweet potato pie or our mother's kiss on a cheek, we are time traveling.

As you get comfortable in the place you now call home, remember to tuck those memories deep in your heart because they will come in handy on lonely nights and stressful days and when you need to remember you are loved.

I want to end my writing by expressing a lot of gratitude. First to you, for taking time to be on this journey with me. It is has been a bumpy ride, but I am here for it. And as the "old folks" would say, I wouldn't take nothing for my journey now. I am so thankful for *Healing: The Act of Radical Self-Care*. It has allowed me to color outside of the lines, for my poetry to not rhyme, for my songs to be off-key, and for my colors to not match. It's okay that Orange does not go with everything, but healing and radical self-care make room for all of it. It is a wonderfully messy and colorful proposition. It allows for folks to enter at different points, to rest and not quit, to run fast, jump high, eat well, and to raise hell, and then do it all over again. It makes room for time travel and forbidden love and imperfect families, and for cousins, hee-hawing, love and light, the ugly cry, the holding contradictions, and the amazing, awesome, and brilliant.

Radical self-care gives you space to take a deep breath and remember you are worth it.

Healing is an open love letter to you and to us to remind you that you are loved and worth taking exquisite care of. You are worth it; it is your right. You are worth loving, forgiving, hugging, and gently correcting. You are not alone. You are indeed amazing, awesome, and brilliant. Don't give up on me, and I will not give up on you. Let's not give up on the world. We are all we got. Please know you are always welcomed OM. Now go ahead and live your best life!

Acknowledgments

To all who are reading this book, thank you.

The old gospel song goes, "Somebody prayed for me, prayed for me, took the time to pray for me, I'm so glad they prayed, I'm so glad they prayed for me." Indeed there are so many to thank, and I will not list all of the names, for that would be another whole book. But trust and believe, I have a deep and wide love for everyone of you who contributed to my journey of healing and radical self-care.

To the divine, whom I call God, and the ancestors for reminding me that healing is not only possible, but it is the only way through pain to access joy.

To my mom, Jewell Williams Lewis, thanks for choosing to give me life, risking your own and creating a pathway for my life-long healing journey.

To my father, James Lewis, Sr., the best dad ever. I miss your comforting hugs and your gentle affirmations, and yet I still feel your infinite love. You showed me a pathway to possibilities of healing with your beautiful mind and brilliant heart. Rest in Power.

To my ancestors, especially my grandmothers, Ms. Trudy B. Lewis for sharing your brilliance beyond your fourth grade education and how to get a PhD in wisdom, and Grandmother Minerva J. Williams for your unconditional love, support, prayers, and your cherry dump cake.

To the one who makes me laugh deeply, allows me to cry hard, listens patiently, loves me without pretense, my ultimate co-conspirator for love and liberation, the best partner in the whole wide world, Joan M. Ostrove—so much appreciation for all of who you are.

To my siblings—Tony Starks, Jennifer Lewis-Watson, James "Jay" Lewis and Patricia Closson—my first friends, my forever #squad. Thank you for sharing your children with me, so I can have the best title ever, "Aunt Joi."

To my family (aunts, uncles, cousins), fictive kin, my besties, my "husbands," friends, and "the cousins" all over the world, especially in East St. Louis, Minnesota, California, Ohio, New York, Florida, Texas, Michigan, Arizona, DC, France, and South Africa—thank you for taking my early morning calls, my last minute visits, my ask for you to review one more thing, your shoulder for me to cry on during one of the toughest years of my life. I really appreciate it.

To the Frogtown neighborhood kids, the "young Omies," thank you for inspiring me to play and reach for my humanity; y'all have reminded me of what is possible.

To my editor, Dara Moore Beevas, and your amazing team at Wise Ink Publishing, thank you for the VIP service and commitment to excellence. You and your team supported me to get this important work out to the world and for that I am forever grateful.

To my amazing book cover illustrator, Jena Holliday of Spoonful of Faith, thank you for capturing the healing presence I wanted people to feel when they look at and hold the book.

To the OM Team at Joi Unlimited (business manager and administrative support folks) and my OMies (coaches)—what a great team, I am fortunate to have each of you and our growing community. "Teamwork makes the dream work."

Finally, to all the amazing communities and lovely souls with whom I have sat in healing circles, held space for tough negotiations, mediated intense conflicts, and the community of healers, co-conspirators, activists, families and loved ones in the fight for liberation from oppression, and for those who have experienced so much loss and trauma—I see you, I am with you, and I thank you for letting me hold space with you on this healing journey.

With love and light,

Dr. Joi

DR. JOI LEWIS is the CEO and Founder of Joi Unlimited Coaching & Consulting, the Healing Justice Foundation, and the Orange Method. Her work is deeply informed by growing up in East St. Louis, Illinois, and is grounded in healing justice. As a "bodyworker" for the collective body (systems) and individual bodies (self), Dr. Joi (as many fondly call her) is a community and cultural healer who holds space for the discovery of critical pressure points for liberation and healing from trauma through radical self-care. Dr. Joi is a highly sought after consultant, coach, and facilitator of liberation locally, nationally, and globally. After a 20+ year career in higher education, she now describes herself as the "artist-activist formerly known as Dean Lewis." She is an unapologetic joy instigator, a certified Kemetic and hot vinyasa yoga teacher, and a leader of meditation and mindfulness. Dr. Joi believes in interrupting oppressor patterns (including her own) with loving kindness so we can reach for our own humanity and each others'. She has a daily practice of trying to live fully in her own body. She claims the Frogtown neighborhood of St. Paul, Minnesota, as her adult home. You can find Dr. Joi online at joiunlimited.com. Please enjoy this free gift from Dr. Joi: https://joiunlimited.com/hand-over-heart-meditation-landing/